AF375487

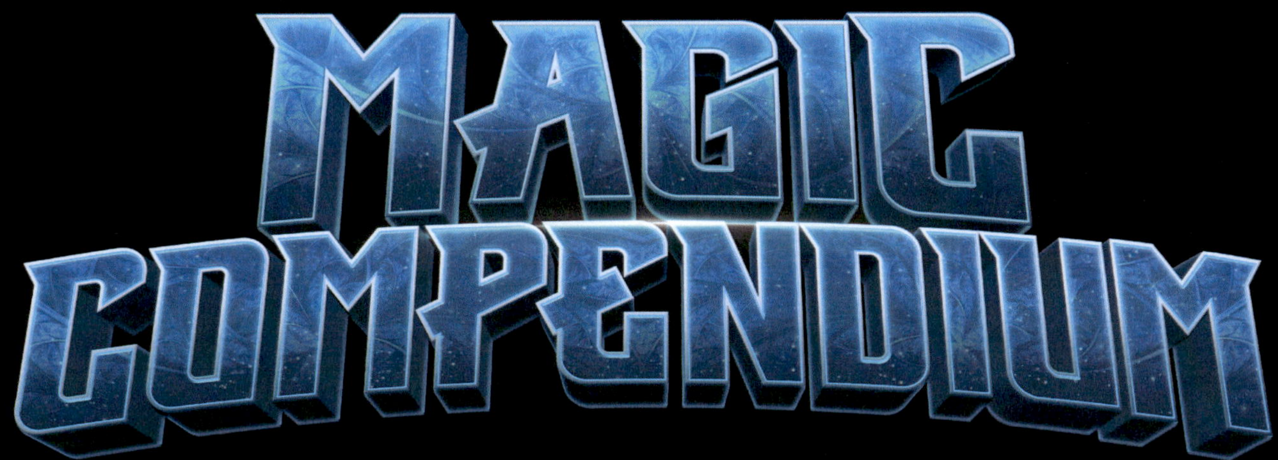

MAGIC COMPENDIUM

Tales of Illuminaria

David **'DELTAKOSH'** Catuhe

DAVID 'DELTAKOSH' CATUHE
The
ZODIAC
LEGION
Tales of Illuminaria

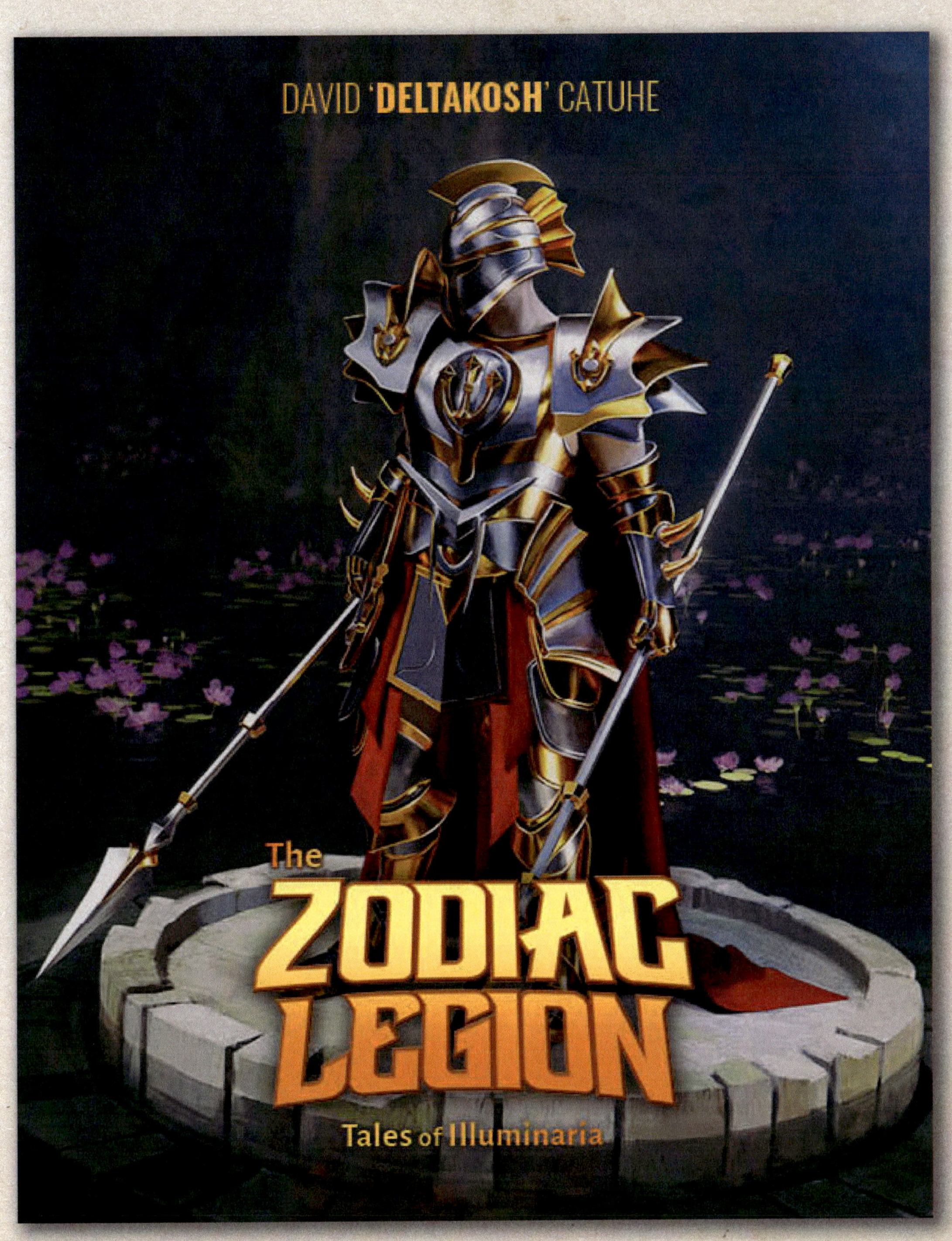

Dear readers,

It is with profound delight that I have accepted the offer to write this preface for the latest edition of the **Compendium of Magic**. Having served for many years as a telekinesis professor, I continually recommend this work to my students, as it is essential for a comprehensive understanding of the extent and impact of magic on **Illuminaria**.

Several decades past, the gods, through the agency of the **Zodiac Legion**, deemed us worthy of wielding some of their extraordinary powers. As practitioners of the arcane, it is incumbent upon us to understand the implications of using magic. It was primarily for this purpose that the first edition of the **Compendium** was once written.

The book you now hold provides an updated exploration of the various forms of magic existing in **Illuminaria**, ranging from the simplest to the most esoteric. It will also help you understand that magic is not a right but a gift that must be earned. Finally, it will enlighten you on the fact that we are still far from understanding all facets of the arcane that the gods allow us to manipulate.

I extend to you, therefore, an invitation to delve into this **Compendium** with an inquisitive spirit, a thirst for knowledge, and a humble deference to the divine forces of **Illuminaria** .

This journey through the history and practice of magic will, I hope, be a rewarding and enlightening experience.

Bel Gelock, Head of the Telekinesis Department at the Nymris School of Magic.

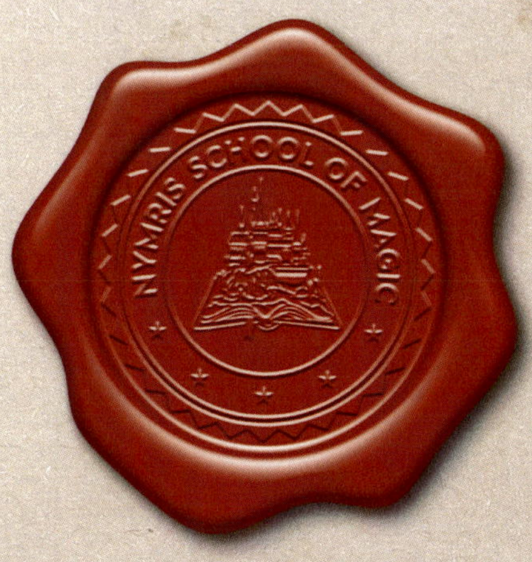

HUMANITY AND
MAGIC

Sixty-five years ago (at the time of this edition's publication), only the **Zodiac Legion** held sway over the magic bestowed by the gods, relegating the rest of humanity to mere spectators. Occasionally, however, some individuals could commune sufficiently with **Illuminaria** to establish a connection and touch the source of magic. This was known as wild magic – an unbridled form that typically had little impact on the environment.

Various theories were tested to unravel the workings of this wild magic. Some predicted that honoring the gods was necessary to earn their favor, but this thesis was quickly abandoned because the **Legion** was clear on the matter: the gods did not require devotion. They existed beyond human desires and needs, eschewing manifestation through mere *"believers."*

The most rigorous inquiry was conducted by **Aaran Nesh**, subsequently the dean and progenitor of the Telekinesis School in **Port Arhoc**. He drew a direct correlation between the presence of mana pyramids and the ability of wild magic practitioners to establish a link.

But even with this valuable information, no human managed to harness magical manipulative prowess to rival that of the **Legion**.

The key came from the **Legion** itself. One day, they decided to convene the foremost luminaries in magical research at the **Nymris** conclave, laying the foundation for the diverse magic schools of **Illuminaria**.

The impetus behind this decision remains shrouded in ambiguity even today. However, it is commonly accepted that the gods agreed that humanity had evolved sufficiently and was ready to understand the power and responsibilities inherent in manipulating the arcane forces of **Illuminaria**.

The year of the conclave, 3415, thus came to mark the end of the urban era and the beginning of the age of magic.

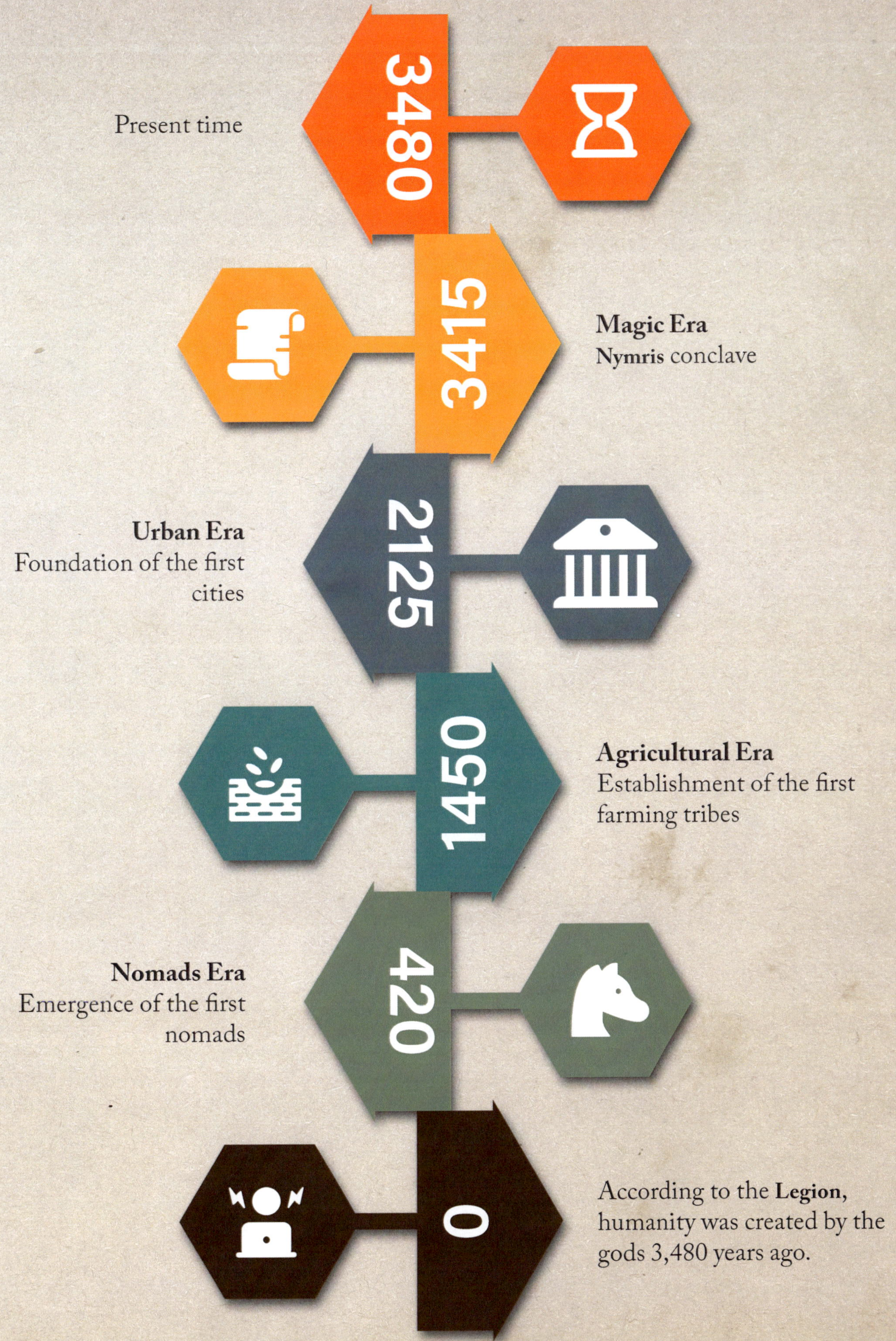

Present time
3480
3415
Magic Era
Nymris conclave
Urban Era
Foundation of the first cities
2125
Agricultural Era
Establishment of the first farming tribes
1450
Nomads Era
Emergence of the first nomads
420
0
According to the Legion, humanity was created by the gods 3,480 years ago.

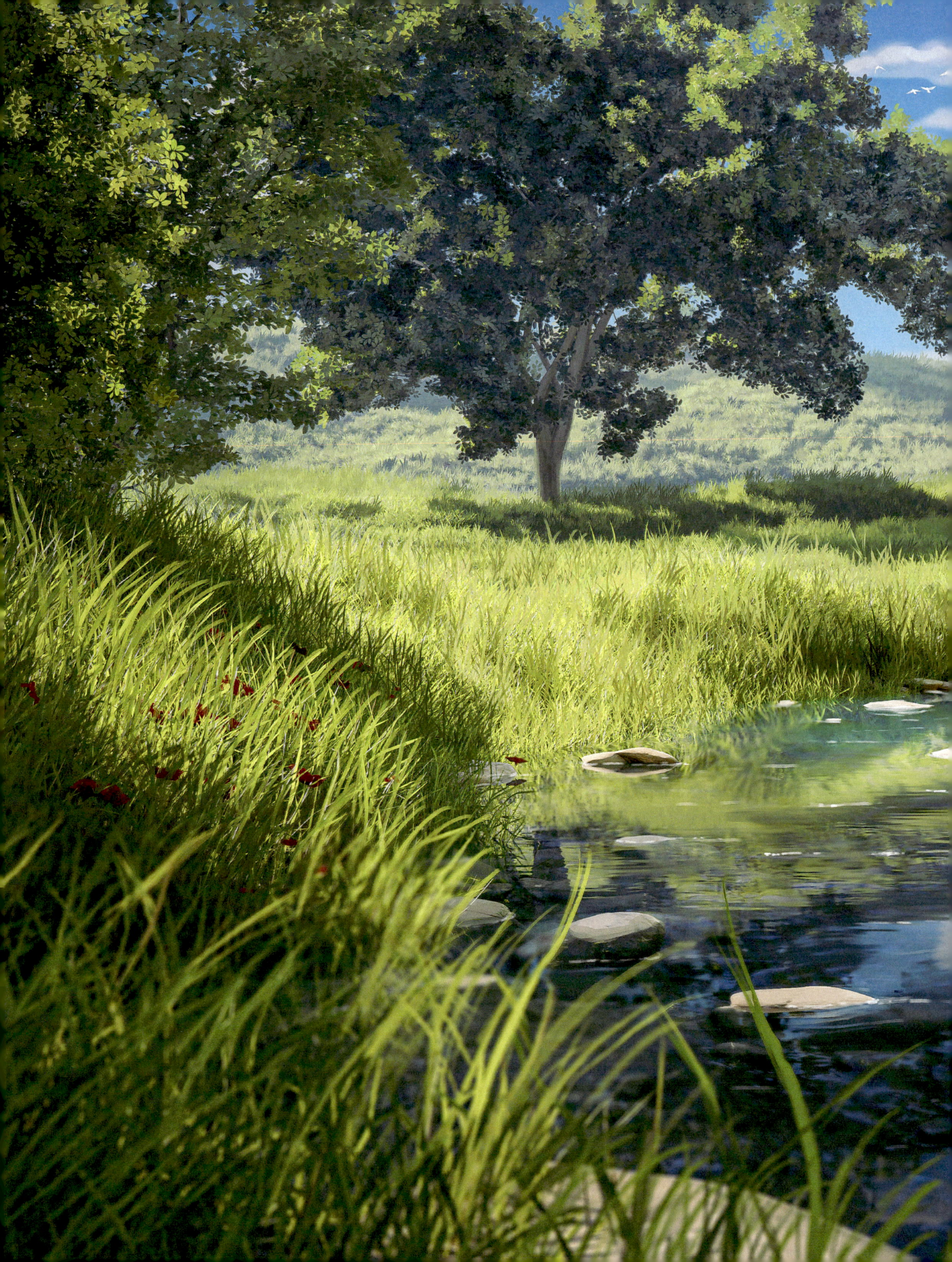

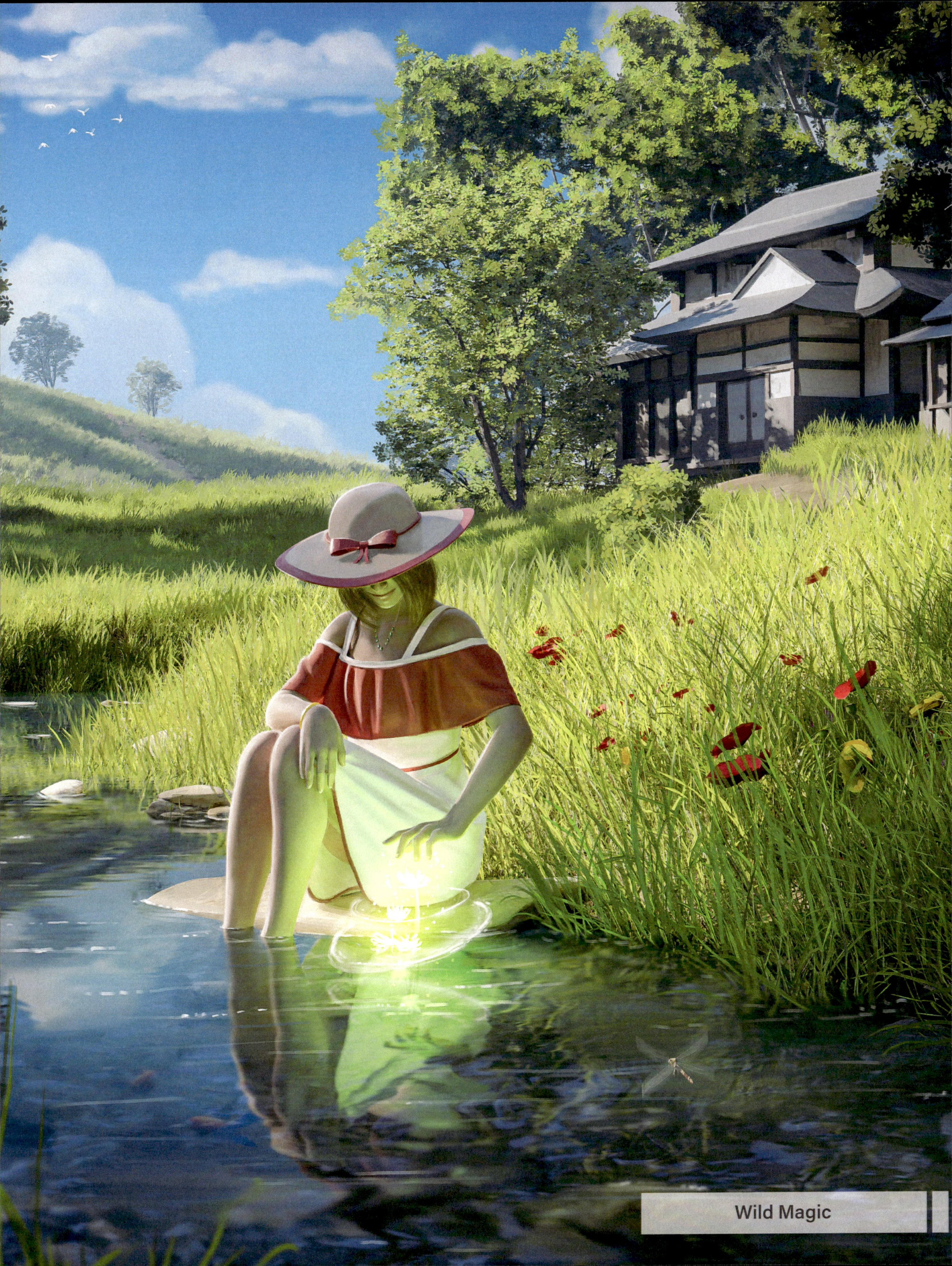
Wild Magic

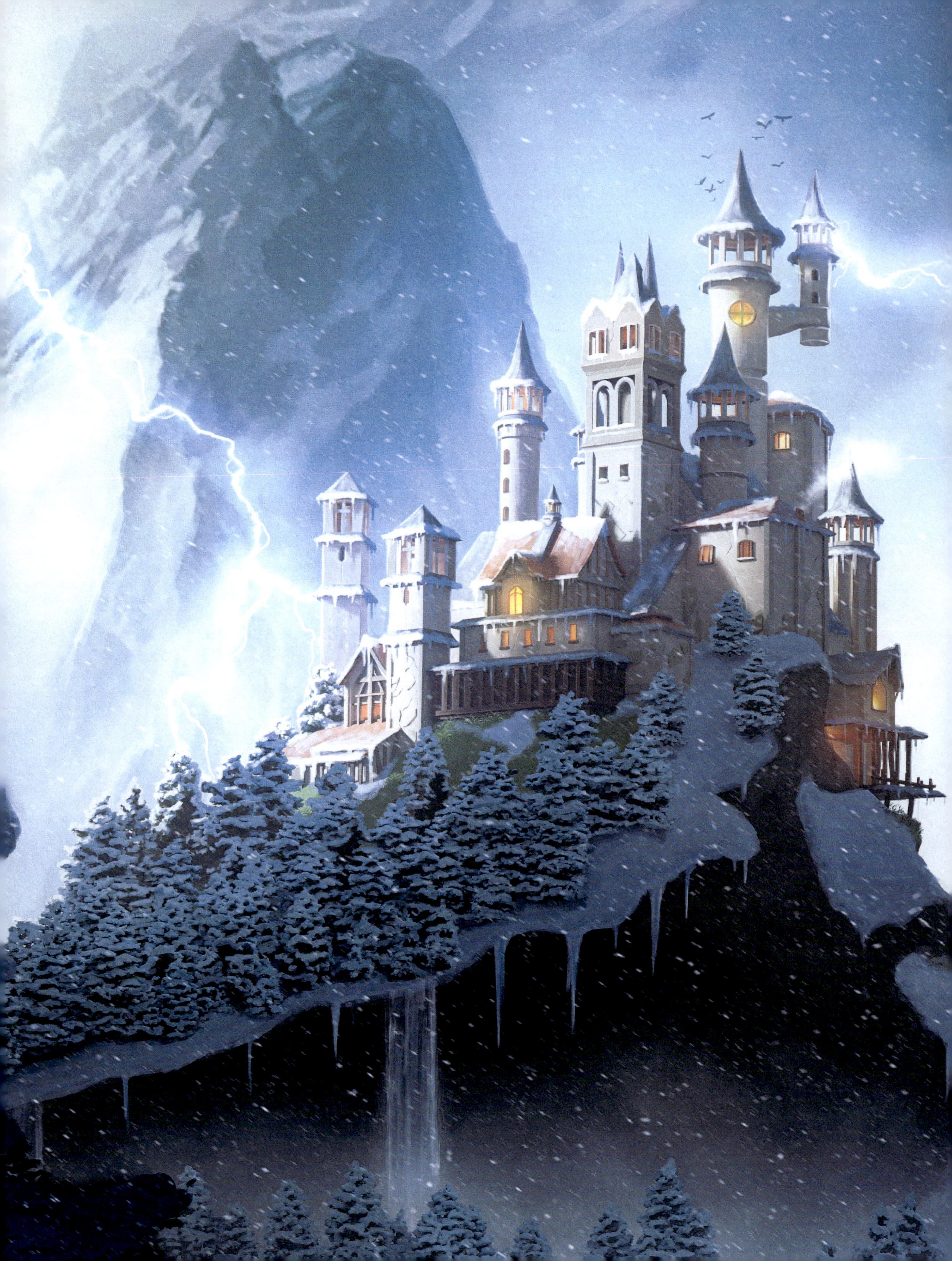

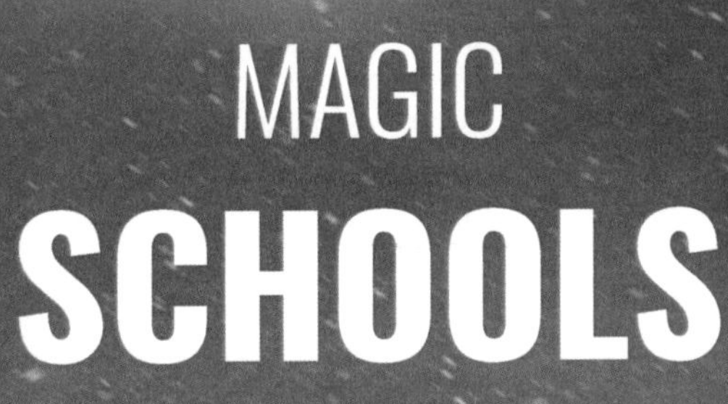

MAGIC
SCHOOLS

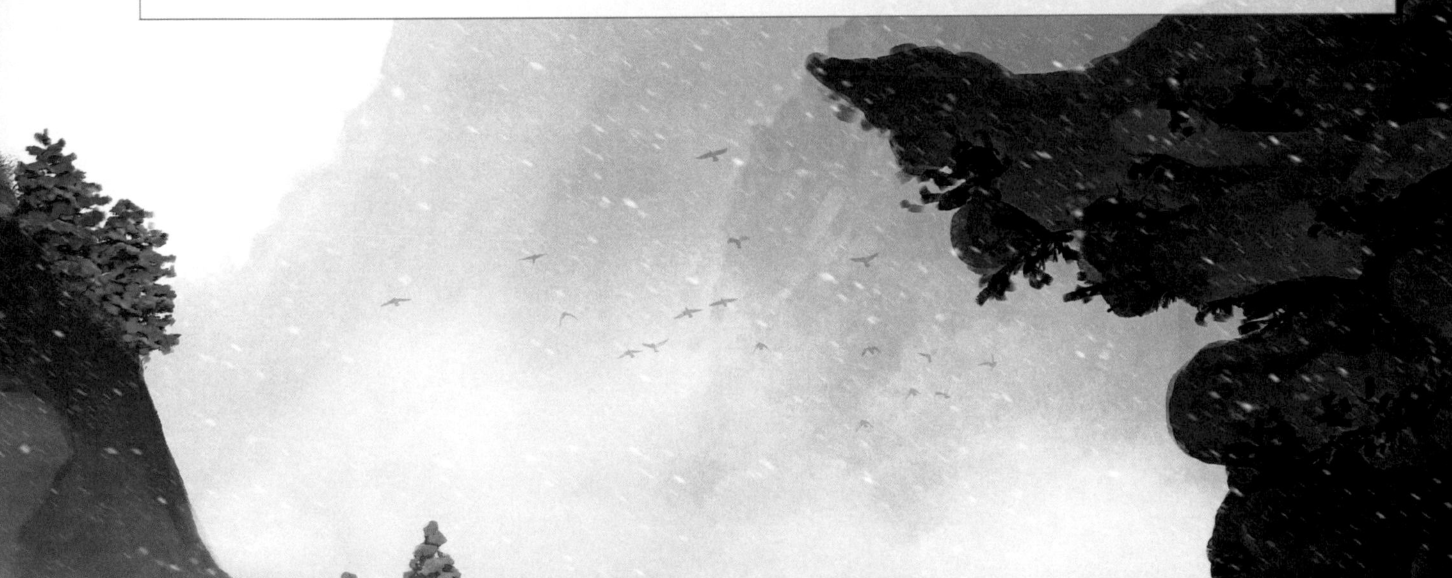

Magic schools established during the **Nymris** conclave were initially led by members of the **Legion**. When the first cohort was finally announced, the knights appointed deans to head each school before taking their leave.

The knights assumed the role of "*consultants*," primarily offering support to the professors, guiding them in the right direction for their research and the formulation of foundational curricula.

Ultimately, nine major magic schools spread across **Illuminaria**, each with a general magical curriculum and, of course, an array of specialized disciplines. Often, the founders of these schools – some of whom still hold their positions today – impart their unique qualities in their teachings.

While unraveling the intricacies of magic and its arcane tapestry, students also delve into more fundamental concepts, such as the pursuit of the greater good and an indispensable tether for forging enduring and potent links with the wellsprings of mana.

Each magic school stands atop a mana nexus, a point of mana concentration in **Illuminaria**, intersecting the influence of several mana pyramids. Unearthed through the endeavors of **Aaran Nesh**, these nexuses provide students with direct communion with the source of magic, facilitating their journey of enlightenment. The buildings themselves, often adorned with mystical sculptures and symbols, are designed to channel and amplify the mana flow.

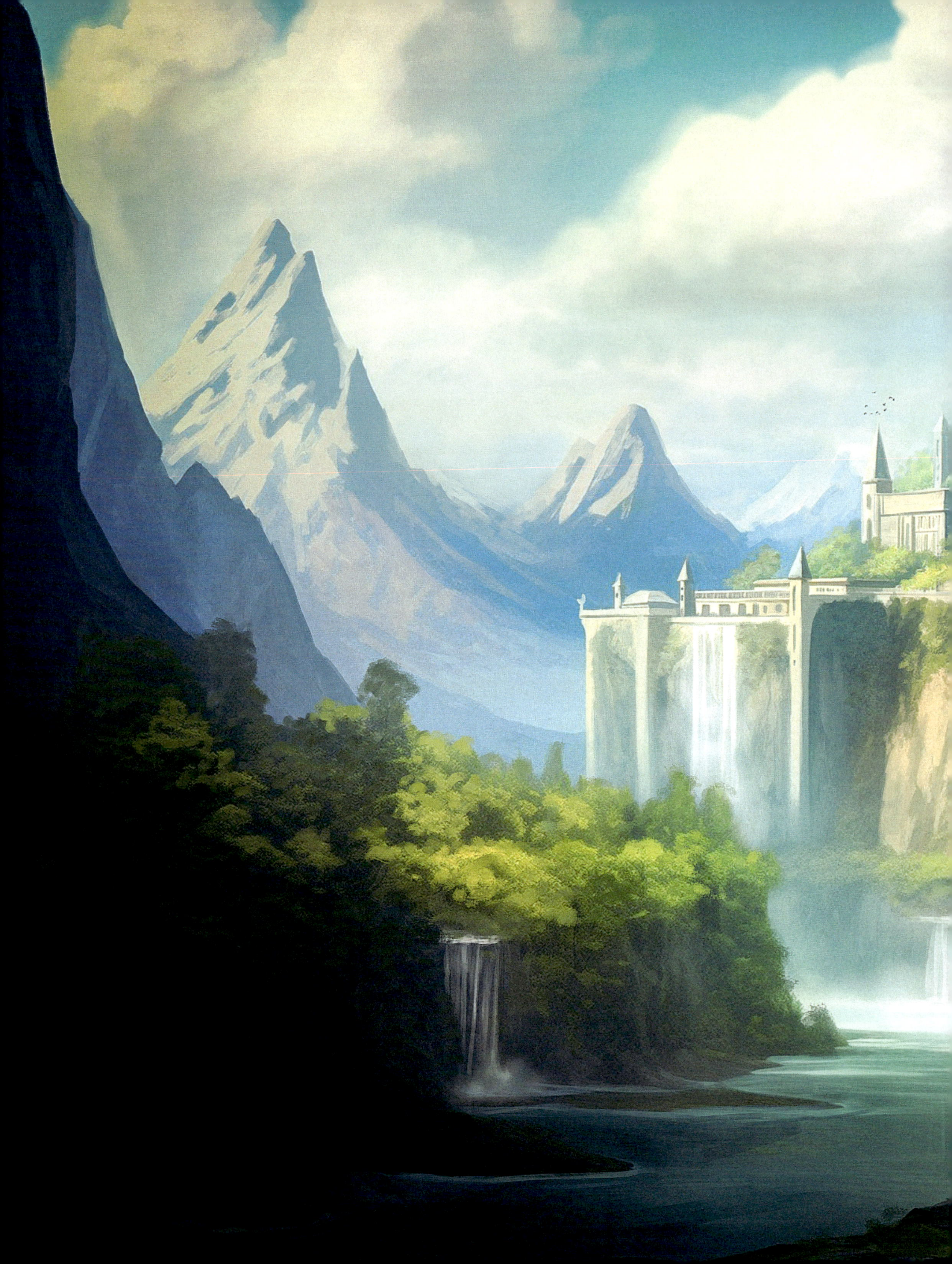

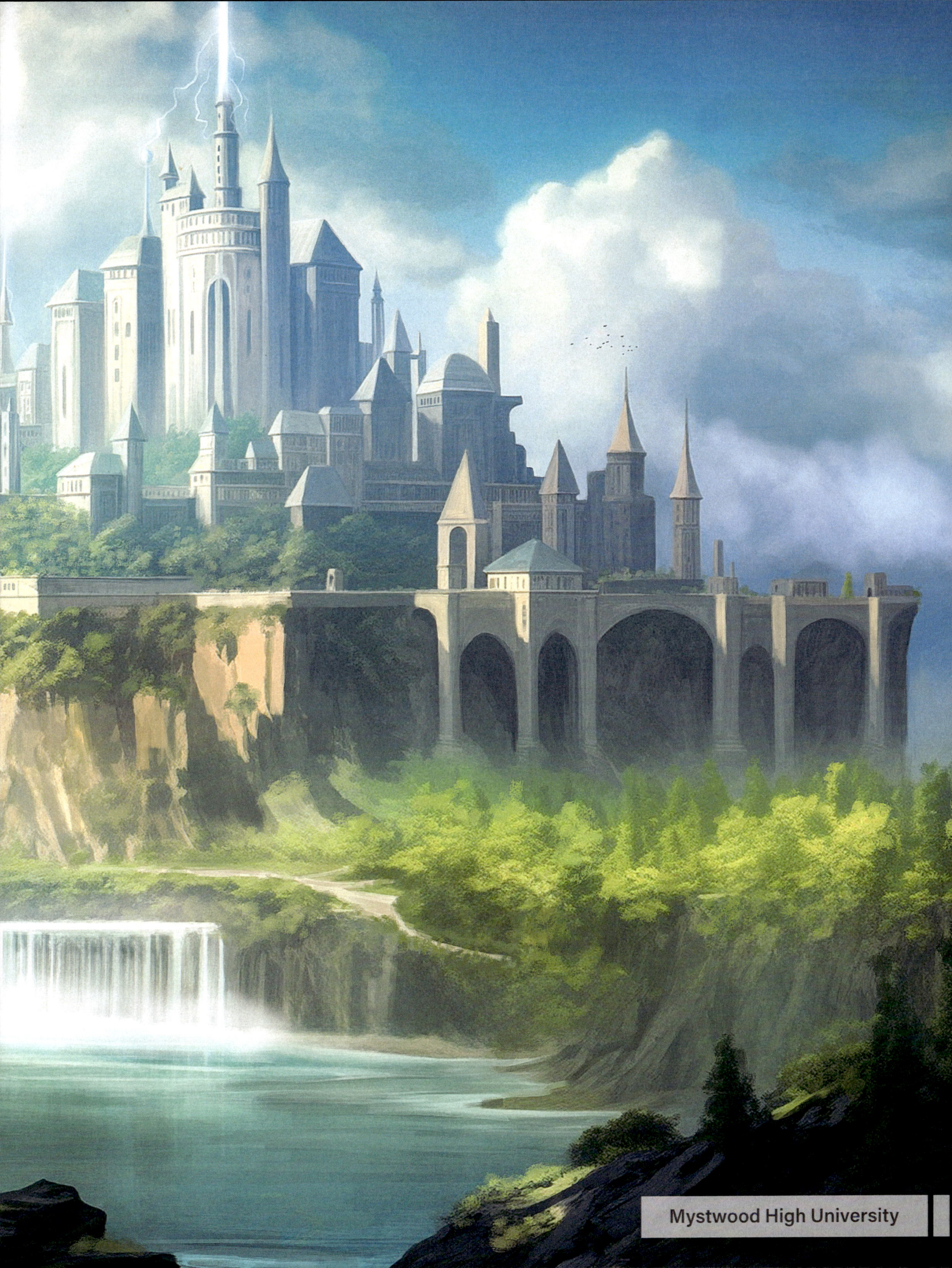

Mystwood High University

POWER
BRACELETS

Each school offers a general magical curriculum that provides a solid foundation in fundamental arcane lore. However, the available specializations enable students to deepen their understanding and skills in a specific magical field, often based on their affinity.

These curricula span several years, commencing with the rudiments and progressing to the zenith of arcane mastery. Students then transition from apprentices to sorcerers or magicians, depending on their specialties. They further advance to the rank of arcanist, ultimately reaching the pinnacle of their studies as archmages, often referred to as grandmasters.

Education transcends the mere transference of knowledge; it endeavors to sculpt individuals who are cognizant of the repercussions of their actions on the surrounding world. Manipulating mana requires significant mental and emotional discipline.

The concept of the "greater good" lies at the core of each school's pedagogy. Students are encouraged to act in the community's best interest and reflect on the ethical reverberations of their magical actions.

When a student achieves the status of arcanist, a special ceremony is conducted. Students are presented before a member of the **Legion**, who awards them their power bracelet – a recognition of the gods' trust and the journey taken to master the magical arts.

These bracelets, however, transcend mere ornamentation, serving as conduits for the remarkably precise and potent manipulation of mana. **Zaniah of Virgo**, in times past, asserted that these bracelets were birthed in the forges of the gods, where the **Legion's** armor, too, found its genesis.

When an arcanist receives their bracelet, they must first synchronize it with their essence. This intimate process is a rite of passage during which the bracelet binds to its bearer, becoming an extension of self. It cannot then be worn or used by another person.

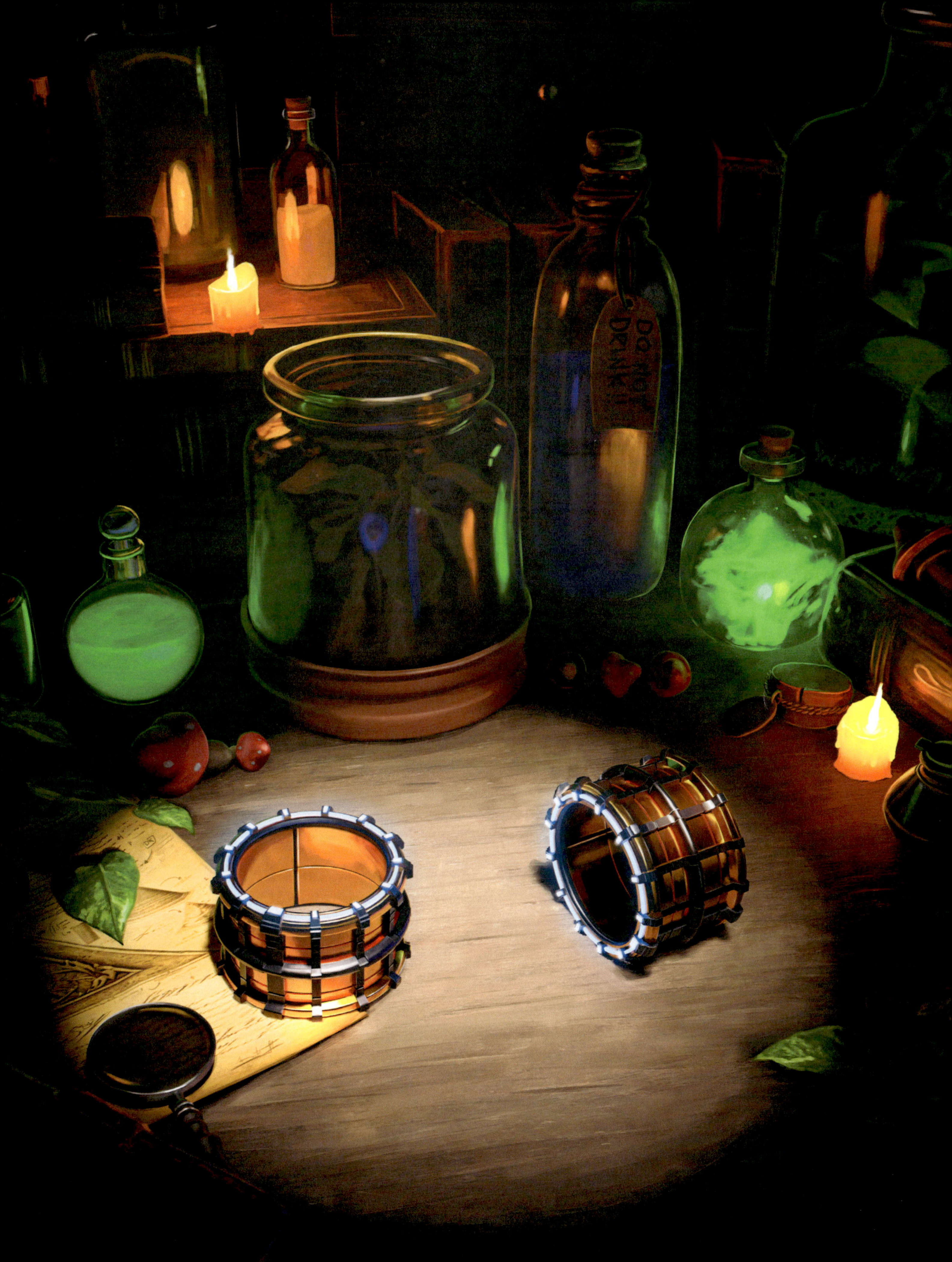

Do Not
DRINK IT

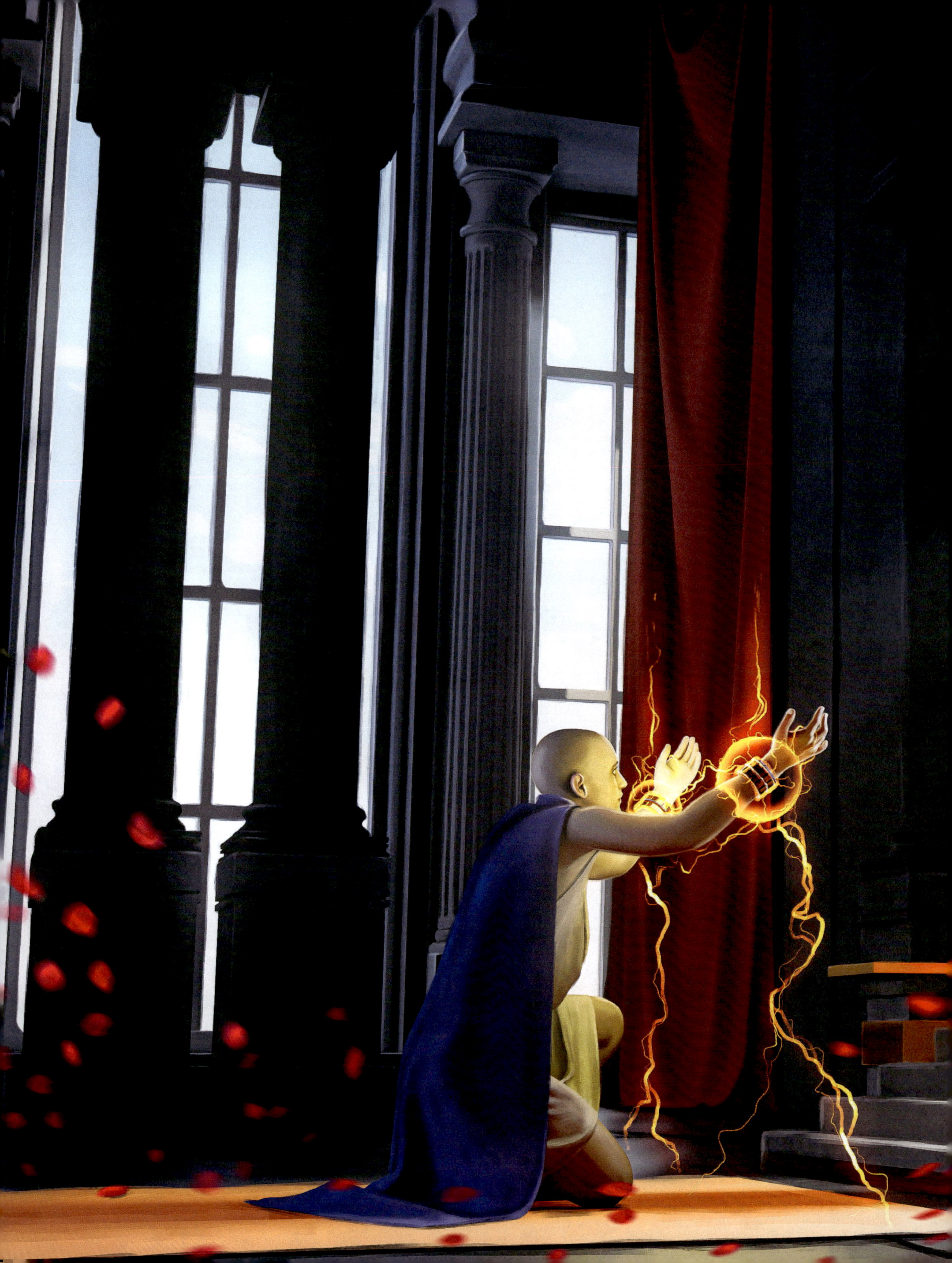

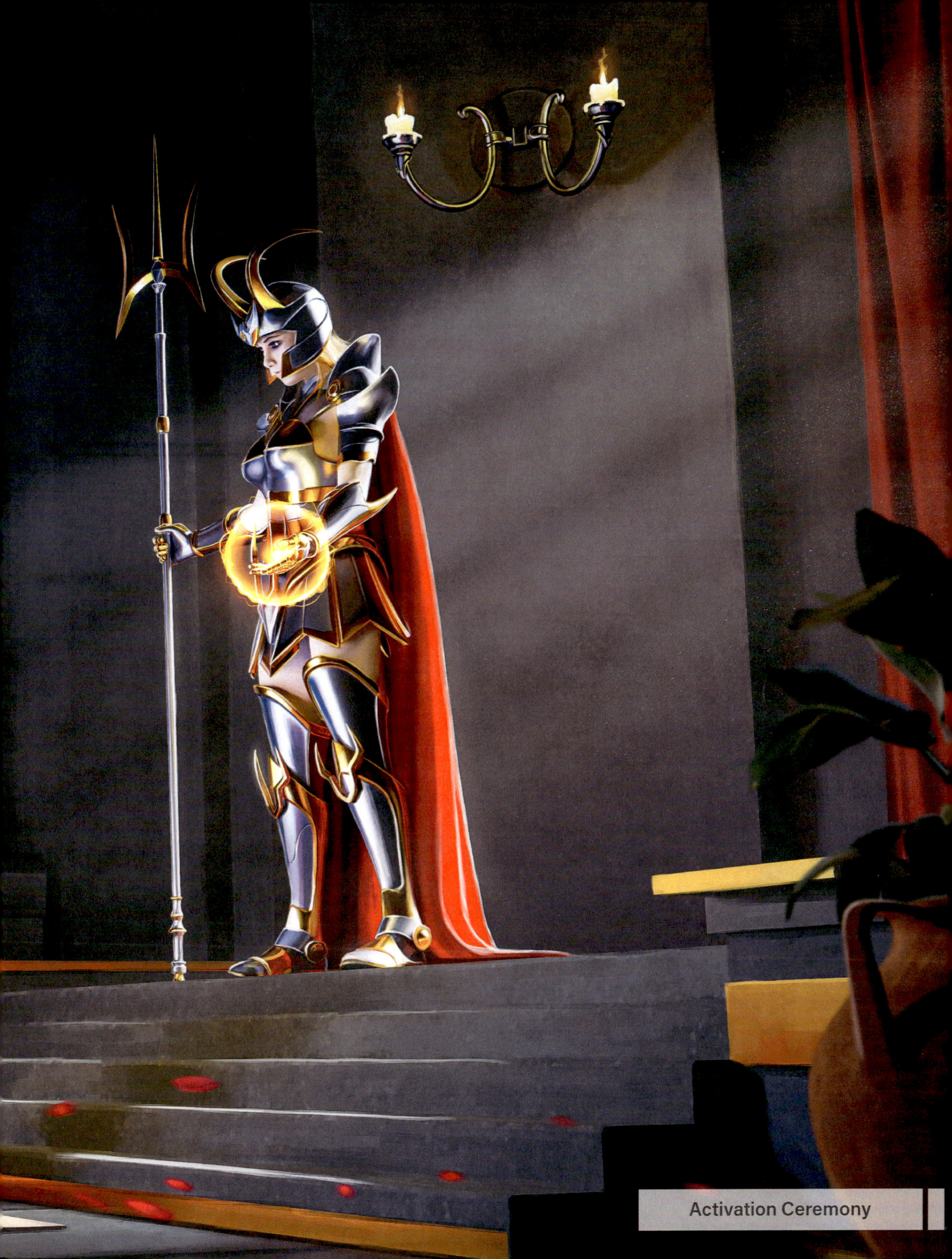

Activation Ceremony

THE 9 ARCANES OF
MAGIC

The schools categorize magic into nine main branches, each distinguished by its specificities, applications, and the mysteries it holds. However, it is crucial to emphasize that these categories constitute only a fraction of the vast spectrum of magic. Indeed, certain forms, including those wielded by the knights of the **Legion**, remain veiled in mystery, eluding our complete understanding.

For instance, it is noteworthy that portal magic was added to the programs several years after the inception of the schools due to a renewed interest expressed by several grand archmages.

Unlisted magics are often so because we lack the means to study or experiment with them, as is the case with sea and ocean control magic mastered by the knight of **Aquarius**.

The same holds true for the ancient magic of the **Precursors**, which, for the time being, remains within the domain of the archaeologists' guild.

TELEKINESIS

PROTECTION

FIRE

LIFE

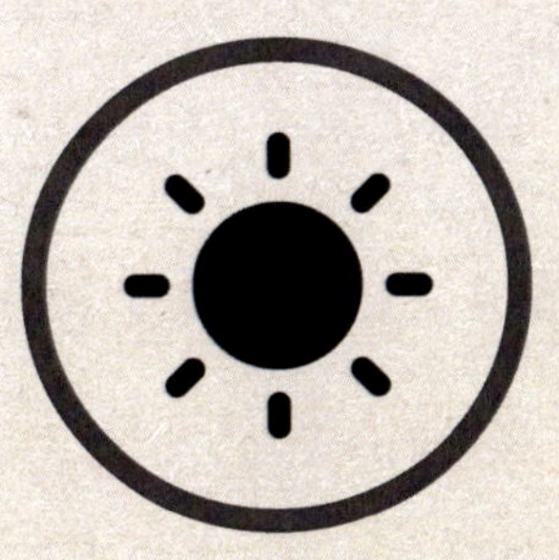

LIGHT

DEATH

NATURE

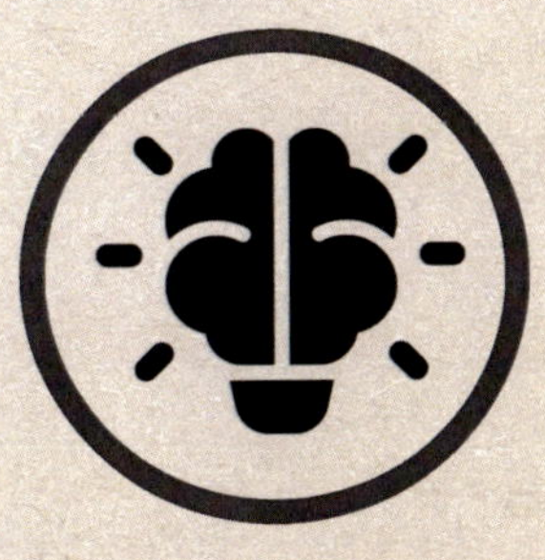

MIND

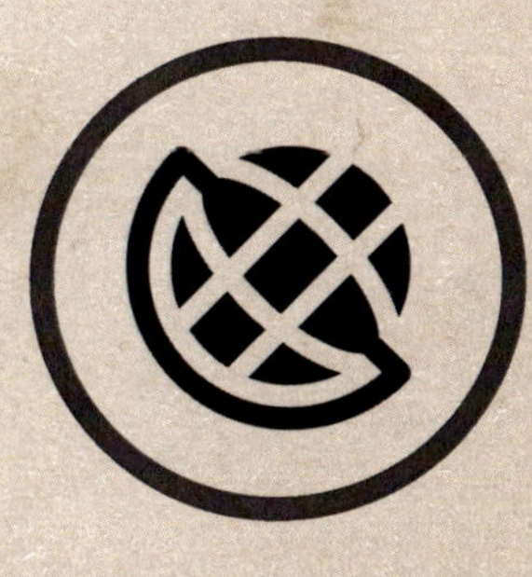

PORTALS

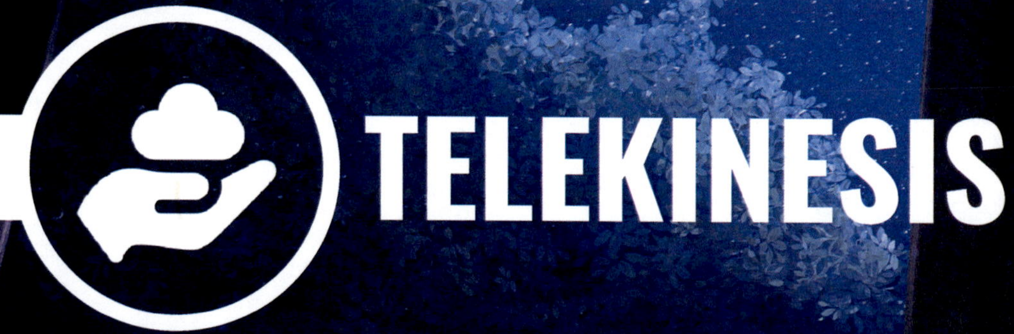

TELEKINESIS

The earliest manifestations of telekinesis trace back to an era when only wild magic was accessible, and only to a select few. Accounts tell of individuals capable of moving objects over short distances (on the order of centimeters) through the sheer power of their thoughts, without any physical contact.

Aaran Nesh was the first to study this form of magic in earnest. Through his research, **Nesh** unveiled the incredible potential of this discipline, later becoming the dean and founder of the **Port Arhoc** School of Magic.

Any student aspiring to master telekinesis must first grasp its foundation: the connection between the mind and matter. This magical ballet demands unyielding concentration, as it hinges on forging a mental link between the user's thoughts and the target object.

The initial exercises taught in schools often involve moving simple objects like feathers or grains of sand. However, with time and practice, students learn to manipulate increasingly heavy and complex objects, lifting large stone blocks weighing several tons with the aid of power bracelets.

The bulkier or more intricate the object to manipulate, the greater the mental effort required. Therefore, even with the assistance of power bracelets, a telekinesis user must always exercise caution. Overuse of their abilities can lead to severe consequences, ranging from simple headaches to total mental exhaustion.

The applications of telekinesis are nearly limitless. It is used in construction, art, medicine, and even in entertainment spectacles. A telekinesis master can assemble a structure, sculpt a detailed work of art, or perform delicate surgeries, all through the sheer force of their mind.

A collaboration exists between several grand telekinesis masters and the engineering research guild of **Port Arhoc.** The goal of their research is to merge magic with a steam engine to manufacture a flying vehicle. As these pages are printed, the **Telekinator-1** is indeed on the verge of being tested in the **Elven March**.

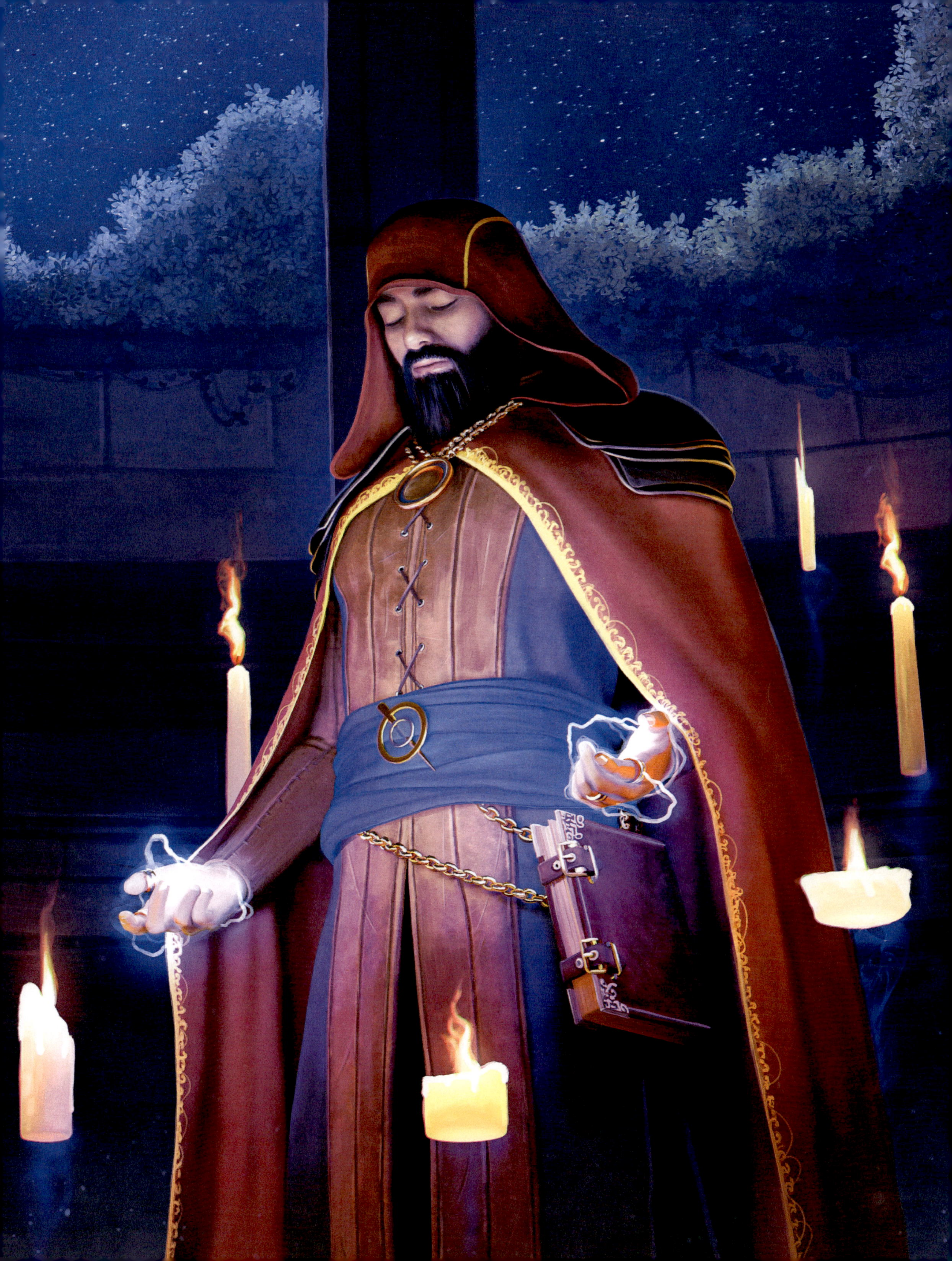

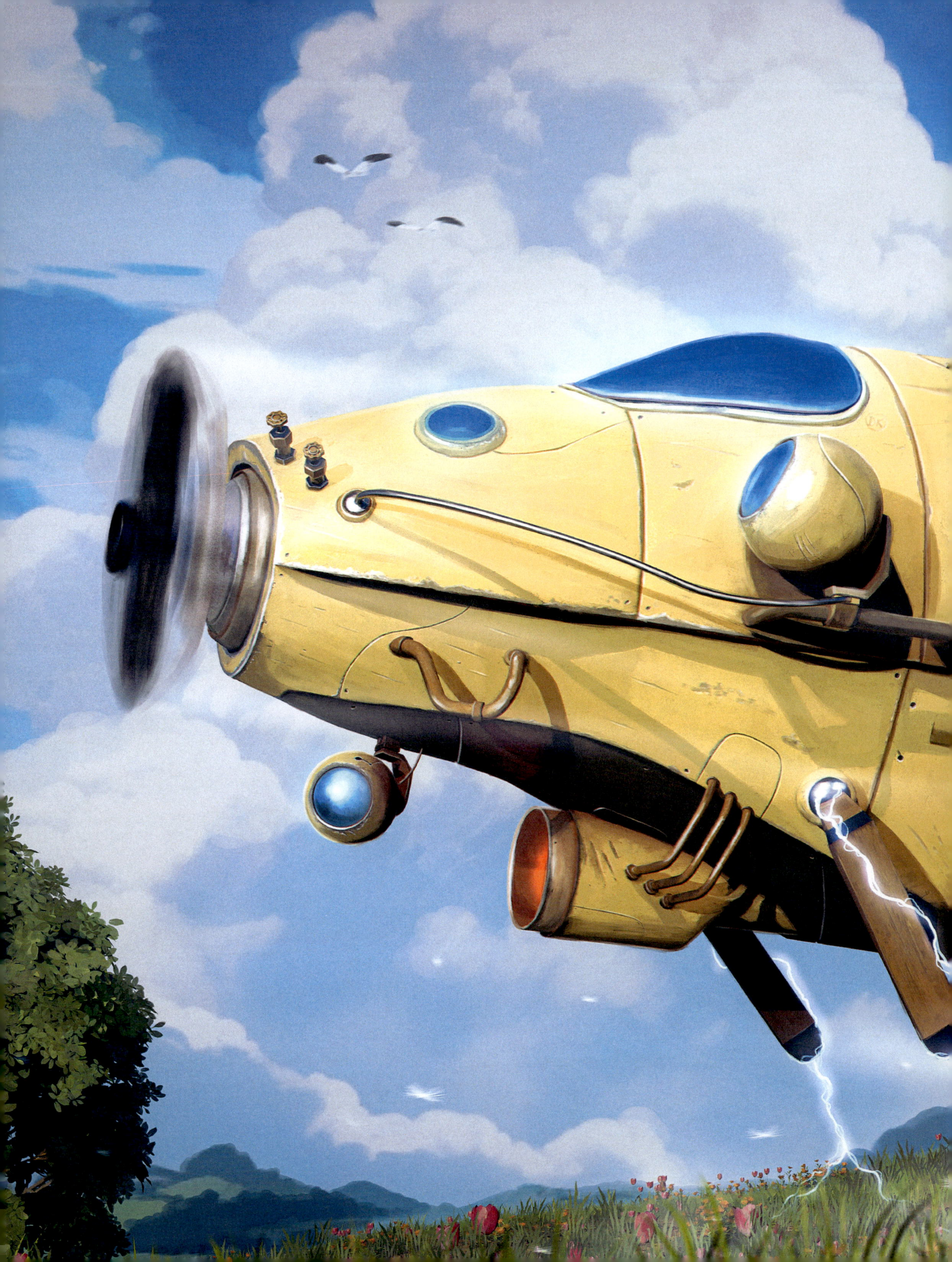

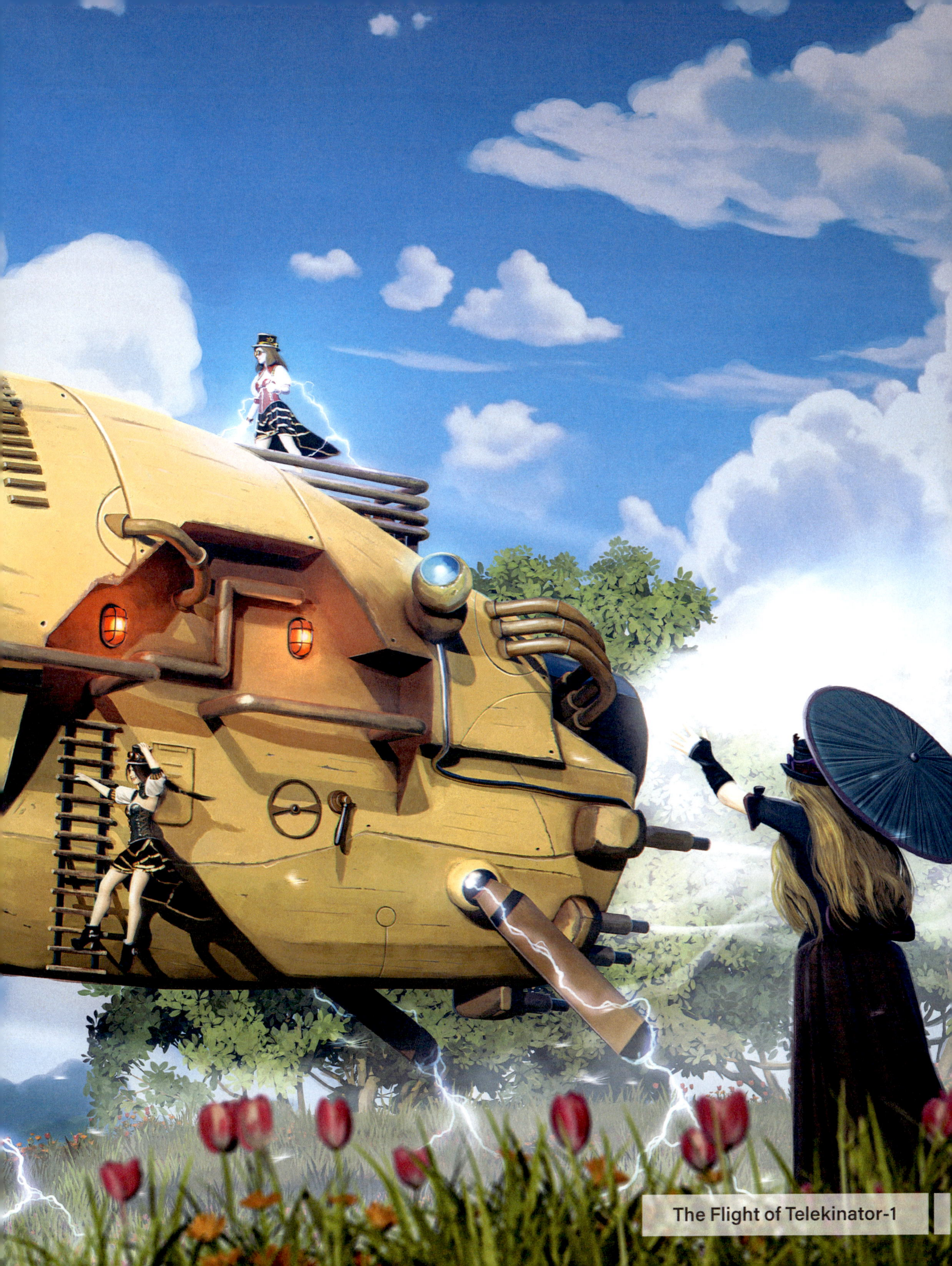

The Flight of Telekinator-1

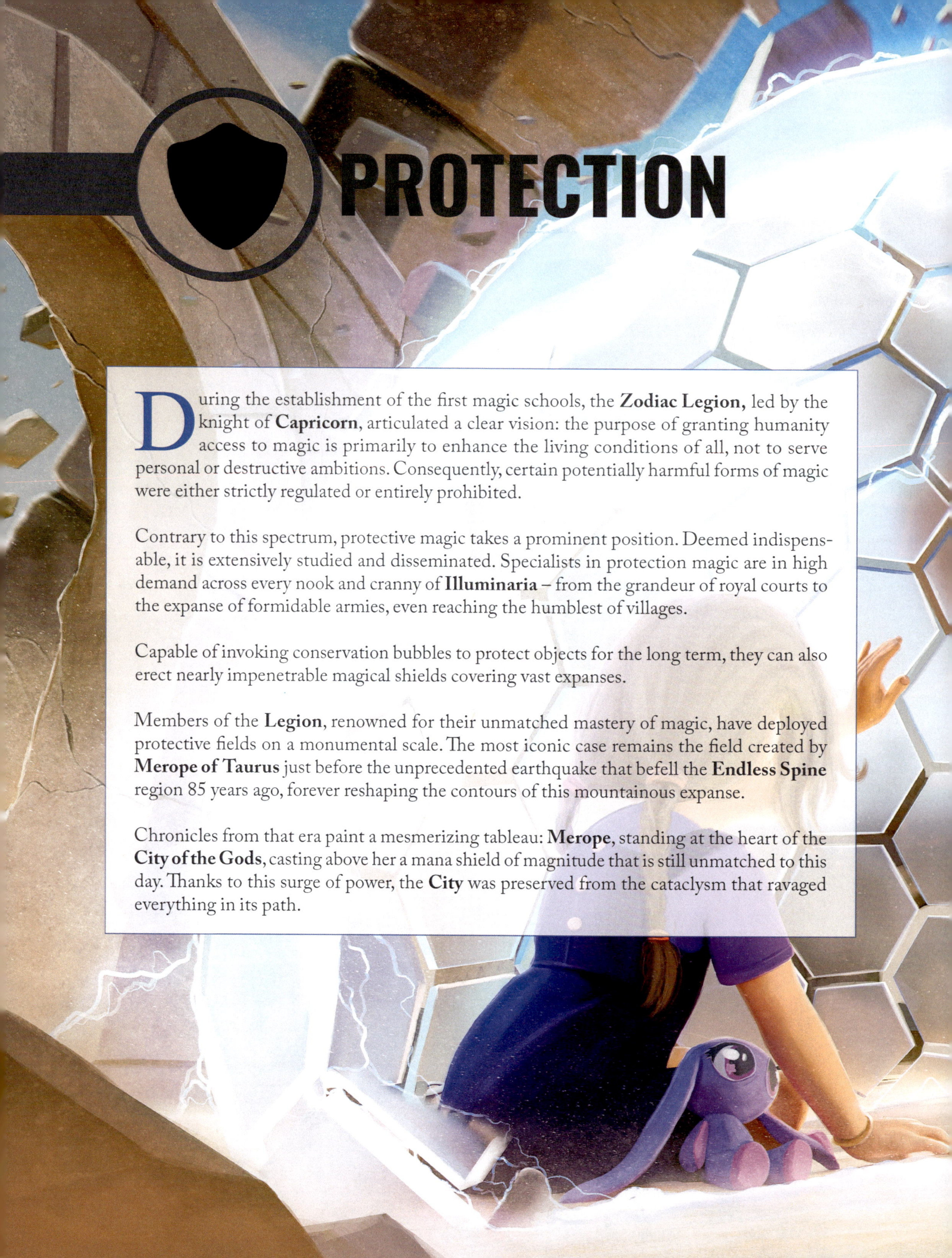

PROTECTION

During the establishment of the first magic schools, the **Zodiac Legion,** led by the knight of **Capricorn**, articulated a clear vision: the purpose of granting humanity access to magic is primarily to enhance the living conditions of all, not to serve personal or destructive ambitions. Consequently, certain potentially harmful forms of magic were either strictly regulated or entirely prohibited.

Contrary to this spectrum, protective magic takes a prominent position. Deemed indispensable, it is extensively studied and disseminated. Specialists in protection magic are in high demand across every nook and cranny of **Illuminaria** – from the grandeur of royal courts to the expanse of formidable armies, even reaching the humblest of villages.

Capable of invoking conservation bubbles to protect objects for the long term, they can also erect nearly impenetrable magical shields covering vast expanses.

Members of the **Legion**, renowned for their unmatched mastery of magic, have deployed protective fields on a monumental scale. The most iconic case remains the field created by **Merope of Taurus** just before the unprecedented earthquake that befell the **Endless Spine** region 85 years ago, forever reshaping the contours of this mountainous expanse.

Chronicles from that era paint a mesmerizing tableau: **Merope,** standing at the heart of the **City of the Gods**, casting above her a mana shield of magnitude that is still unmatched to this day. Thanks to this surge of power, the **City** was preserved from the cataclysm that ravaged everything in its path.

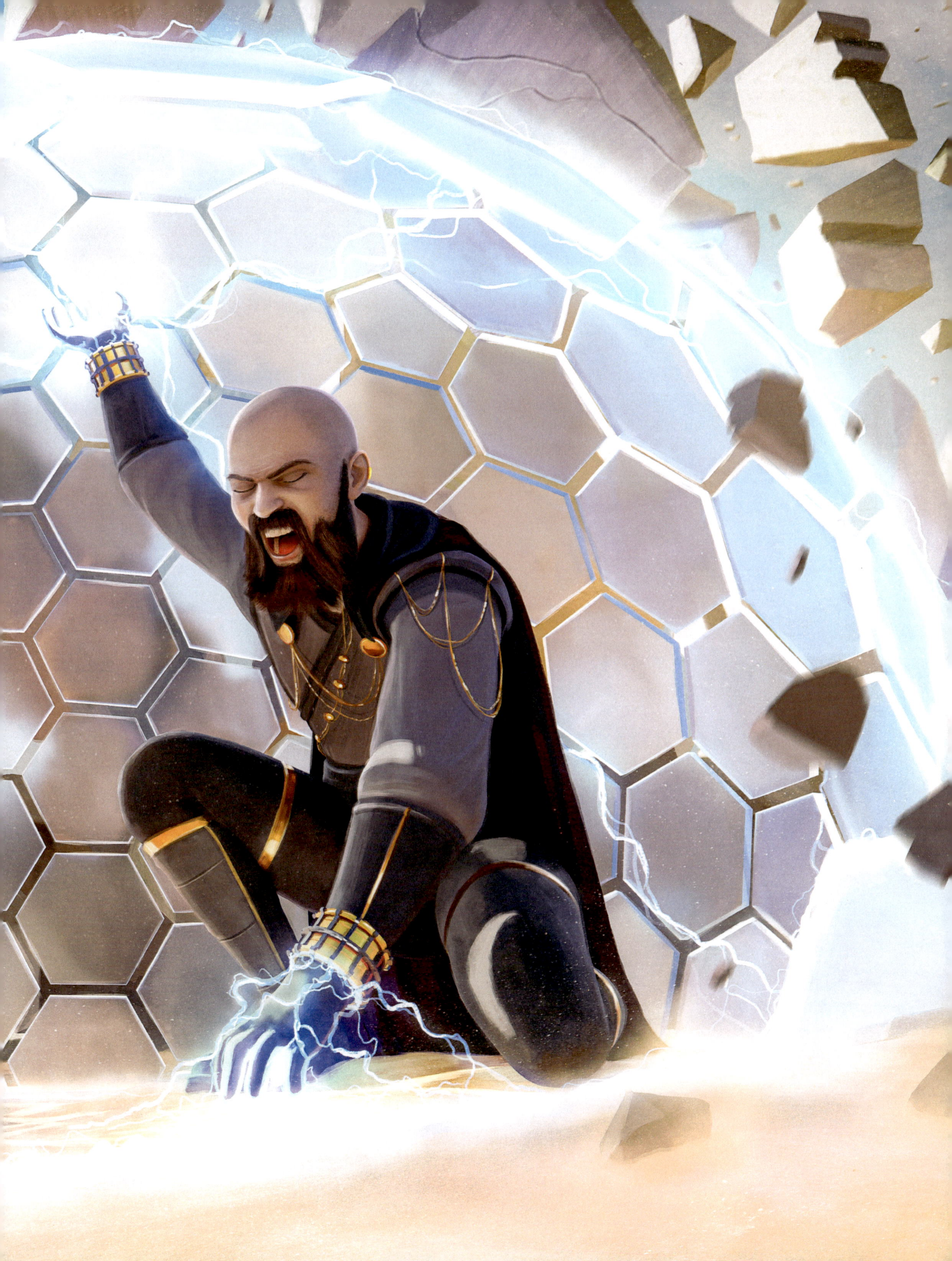

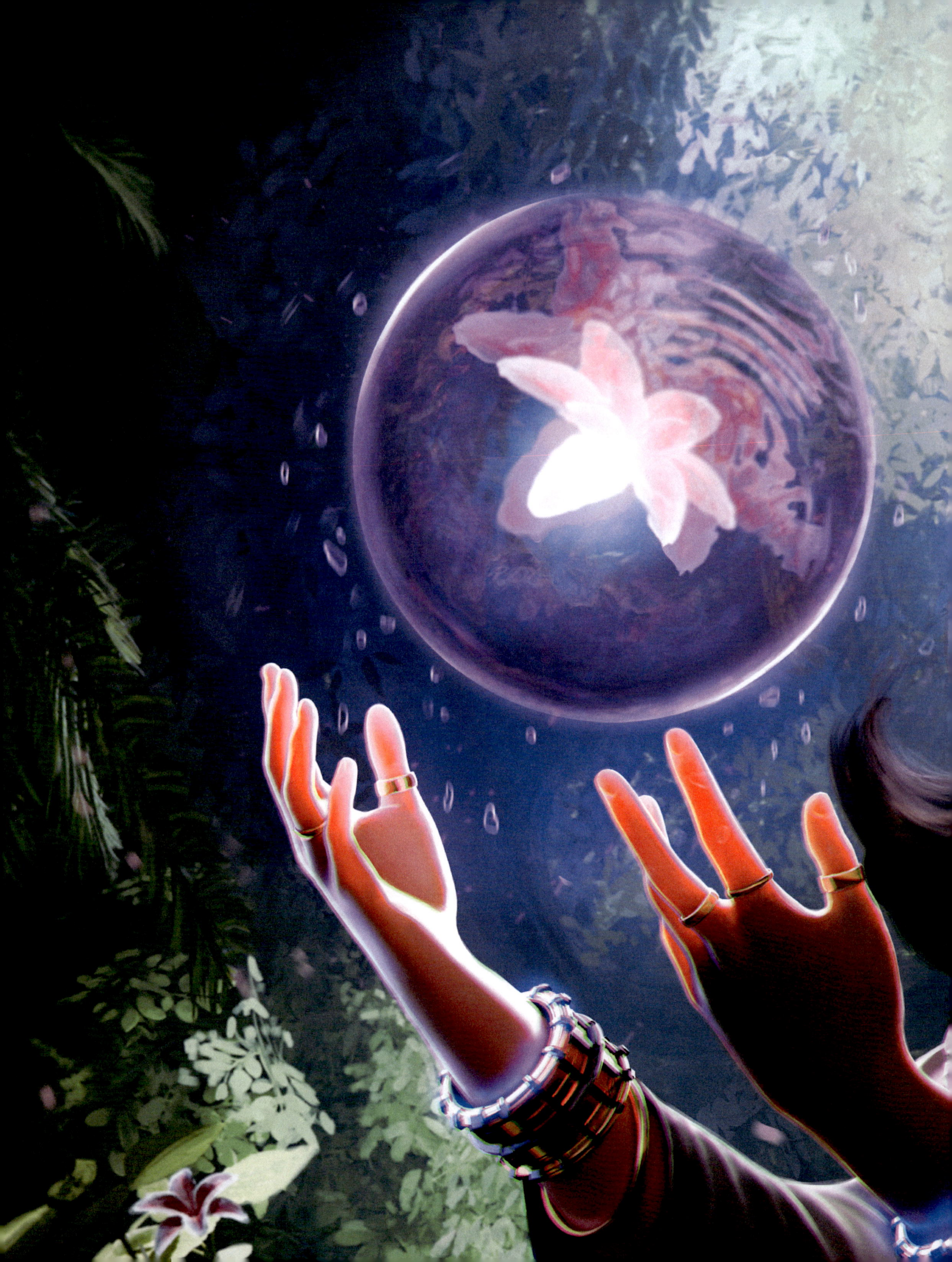

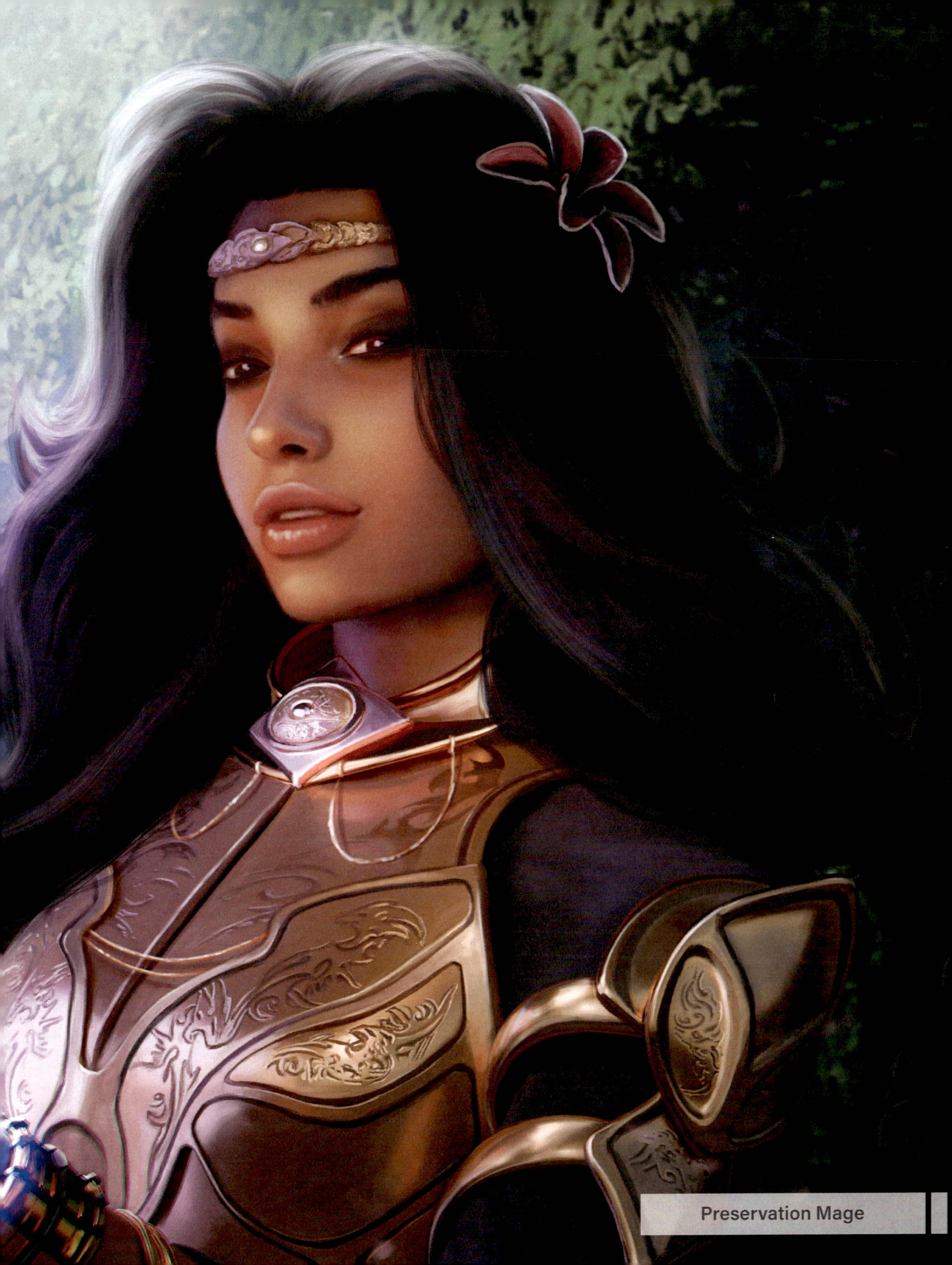
Preservation Mage

FIRE

The allure of fire magic lies not solely in its fiery brilliance but in the enigmatic paradox it presents. Indeed, despite its evident destructive potential, humanity has found itself unable to harness fire magic for combative purposes. The **Vaelinvale** School, despite years of research, stands as a perfect testament to this.

Irrespective of the conjurer's tool or talent, be they adorned with a bracelet or not, the production of flame with belligerent intent remains an elusive feat. This conundrum gains added complexity when juxtaposed with the destructive prowess exhibited by certain members of the **Legion**, **Lion** and **Gemini** among them.

It is the knight of **Scorpio**, however, who embodies the use of fire for the greater good. Her approach is clear: fire, though powerful, should not be an instrument of destruction but a tool for creation. *"Fire consumes, but it also shapes,"* she likes to remind during her visits to magic schools.

A striking exemplar is the advent of arcane forges. Fueled by the magic of fire, these structures attain staggering temperatures, facilitating the smelting of rare metals and the crafting of unprecedented alloys. Through this innovative approach, significant strides have been made in metallurgy, paving the way for materials with exceptional properties.

The takeaway from fire magic extends beyond the fervor of its flames or the oppressive heat it exudes. It underscores the inherent capacity of fire to metamorphose and innovate – a perpetual reminder that magic, in its myriad forms, stands as a catalyst for progress when wielded judiciously and with reverence.

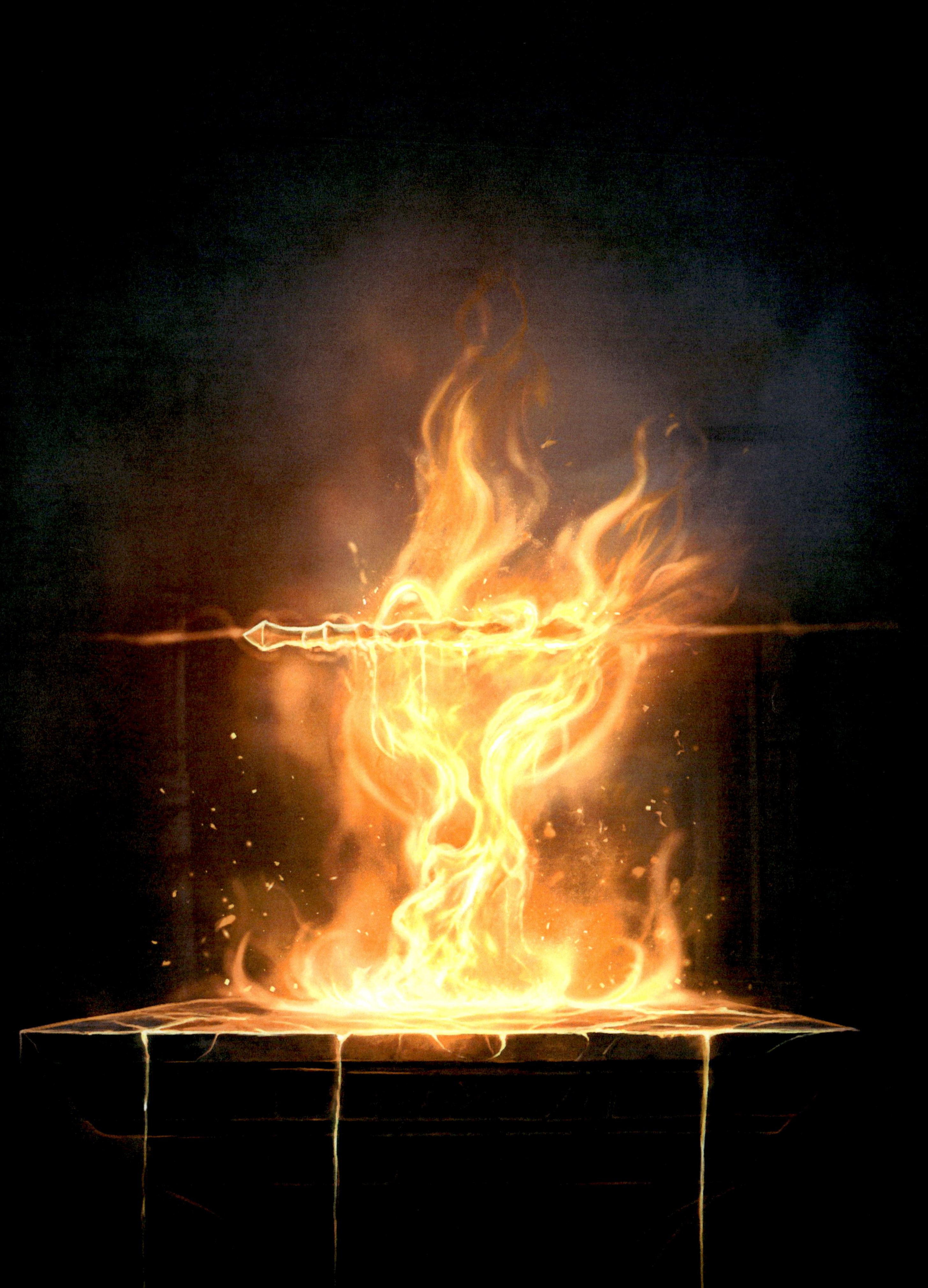

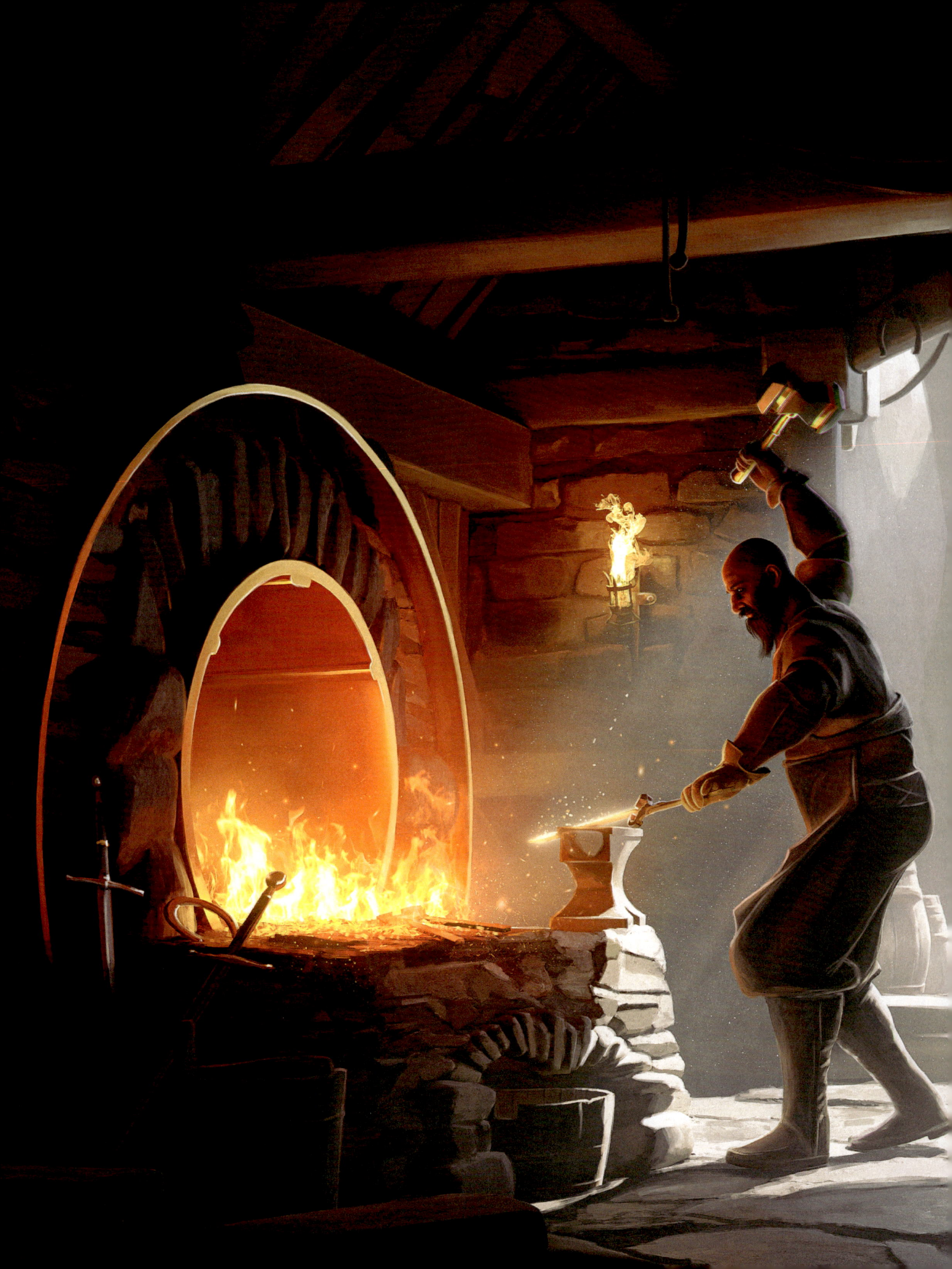

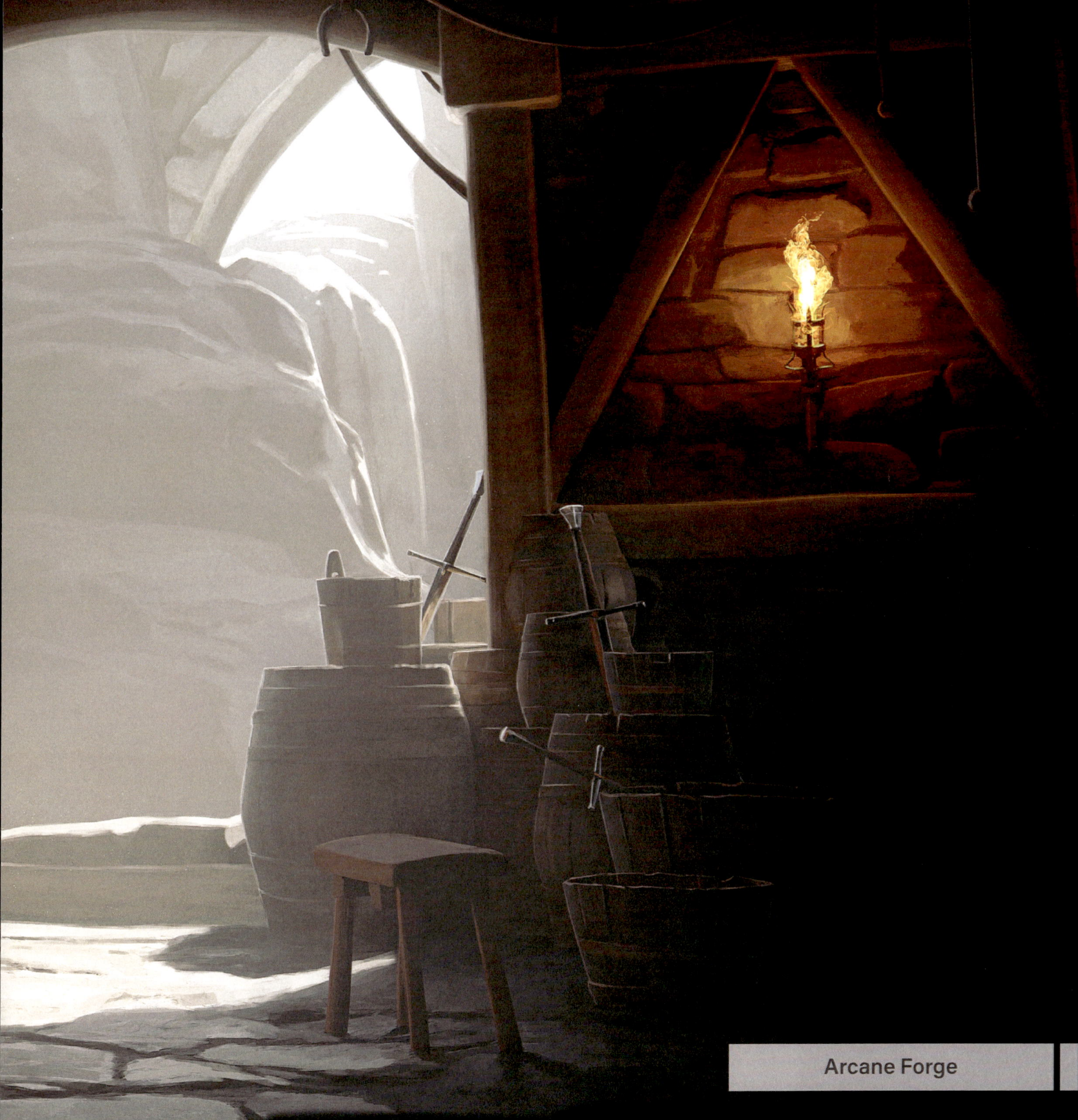
Arcane Forge

 **LIFE**

ife magic is among the most precious. While other forms may dazzle or destroy, life magic brings healing and solace, and above all, it restores hope where none existed. Practitioners of this arcane discipline, often hailed as healers, possess the ability to mend wounds, be they physical or mental.

From deep lacerations to fractures and even intricate maladies, their tender care brings remedy. Their prowess extends beyond the realms of traditional medical understanding, mending afflictions that defy conventional treatments. In the face of medical impotence, life magic takes center stage.

Among these practitioners, battlefield healers stand out. These exceptional mages, trained for the rigors of war, can conjure vast healing fields that enshroud wounded warriors. And in moments, dozens, even hundreds of soldiers regain their strength, ready to resume the battle.

The greatest masters are even capable of bringing individuals back from the brink of death, a rare feat that is shrouded in mystery.

Recently, rumors have begun circulating throughout **Illuminaria**, hinting at the possible discovery of ancient artifacts in the ruins of the **Precursors**. These objects, infused with powerful energies, could apply life magic without the intervention of a healer. The archaeologists' guild has thus launched several expeditions in the hope of retrieving and studying these promising artifacts. If these objects indeed possess real power, they could not only revolutionize the field of healing but also broaden our understanding of magic itself. However, caution is crucial, as these artifacts, in the wrong hands, could have unexpected and potentially disastrous consequences.

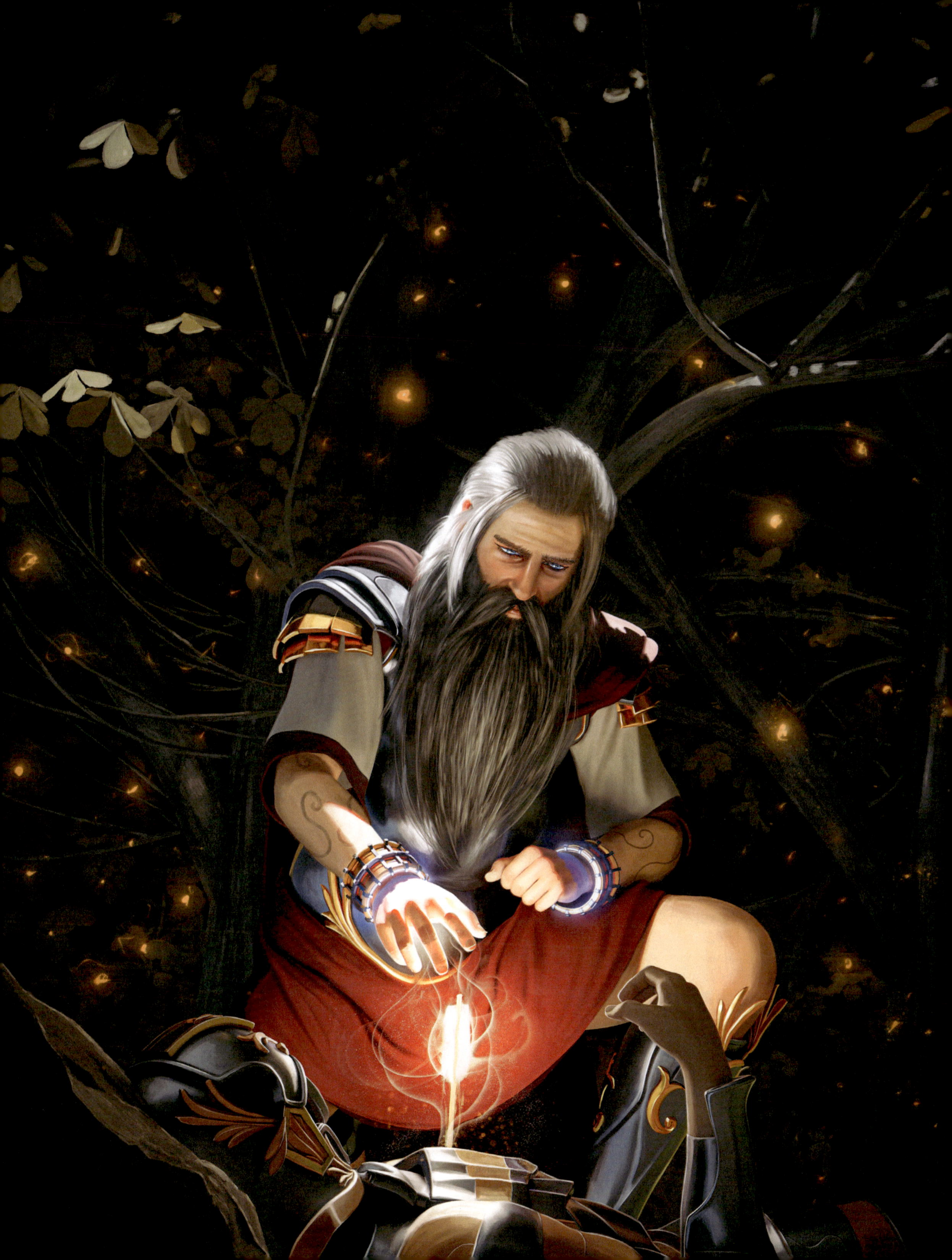

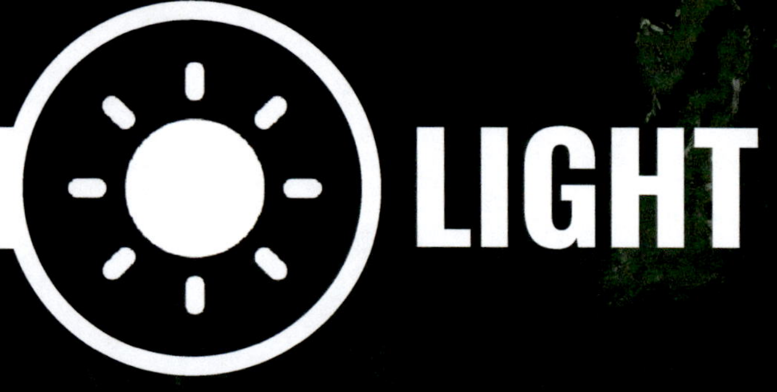

LIGHT

Light magic is often perceived as the most elementary and accessible of all. Its intuitive nature allows for the easy capture of a light source and its restitution as needed. Whether to illuminate a dark path or brighten a room as night falls, this magic provides an immediate solution to its wielders, even in its most elemental form.

Every class of students inevitably discovers the allure of light magic. Its accessibility makes it the first choice for apprentices, providing a sense of efficacy from the early stages of their training. While some magical disciplines necessitate years of unwavering dedication, light rewards its practitioners with tangible results from the onset, kindling their confidence and fervor.

However, let there be no misconception; the apparent simplicity of this magic does not denote a lack of potential. Researchers are tirelessly working to fully exploit the capabilities of light magic. One of the most promising projects involves storing light in inanimate objects. Imagine lampposts that, after capturing daylight, illuminate our streets at night without requiring another energy source. We can also think of jewelry that, imprisoning sunlight, glows in the dark, combining aesthetics and functionality.

The scope of light magic extends far beyond mere illumination. Scholars are already contemplating its use in areas such as security, envisioning the implementation of luminescent barriers to alert of dangers or guide in emergencies.

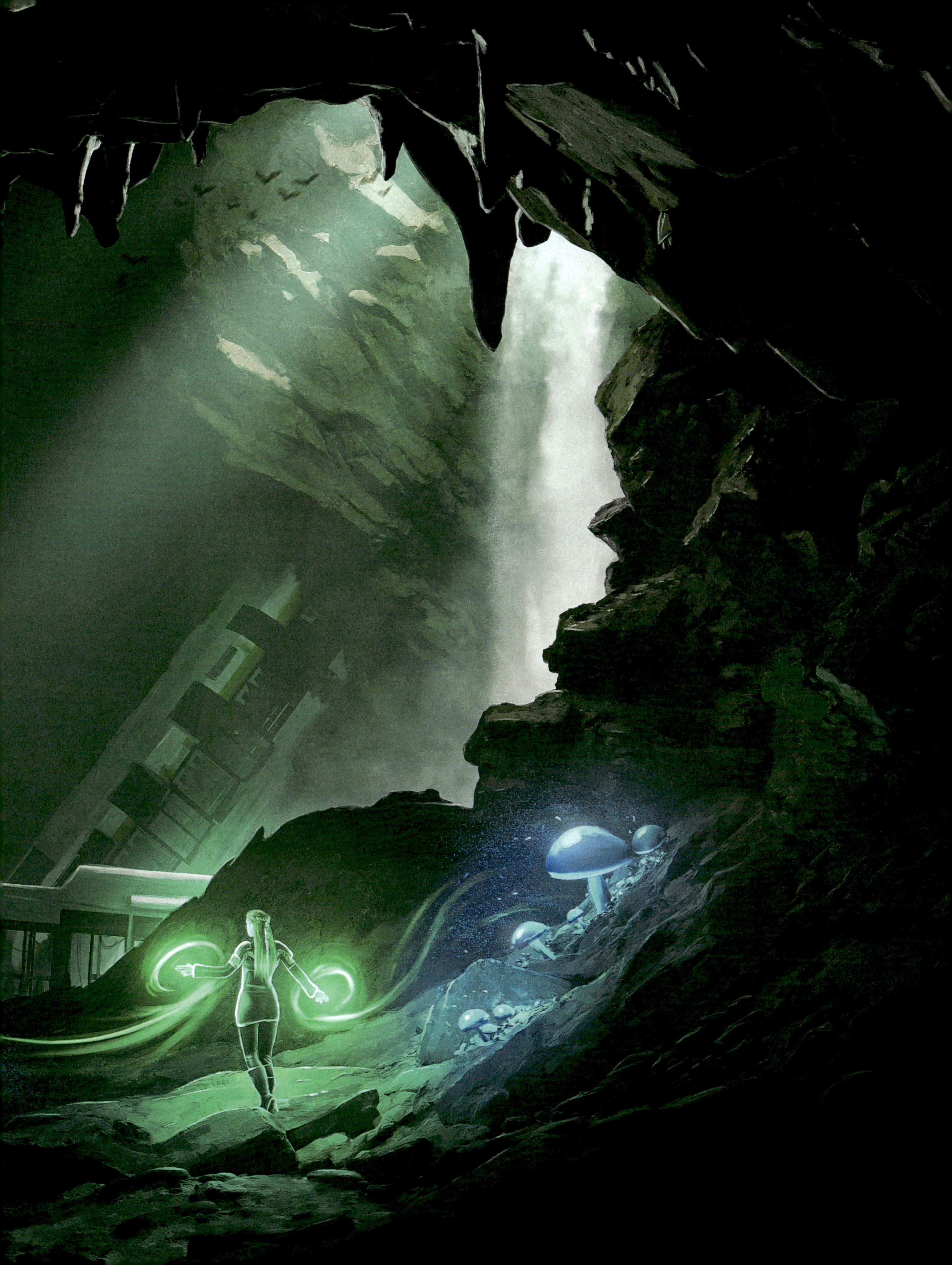

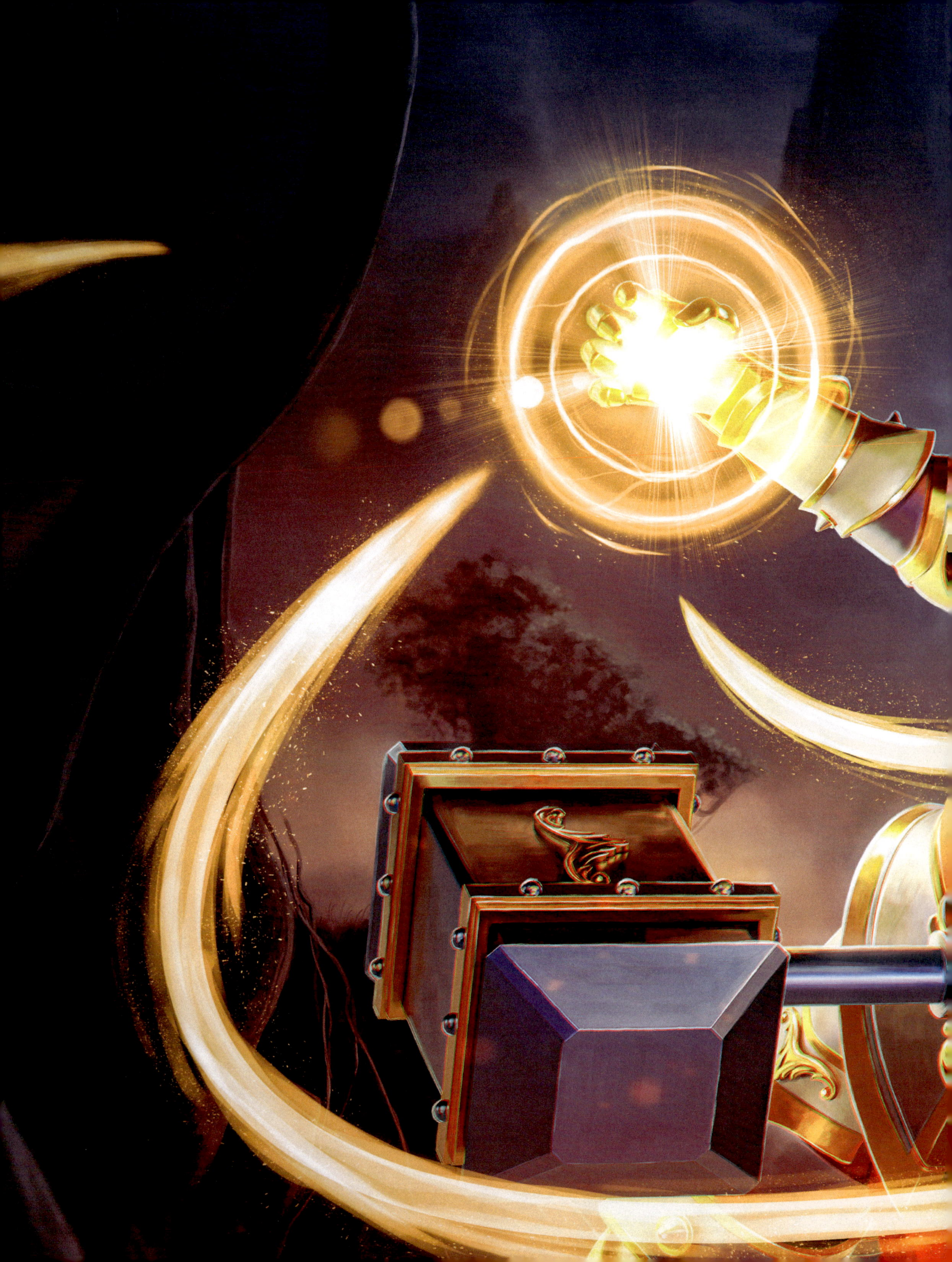

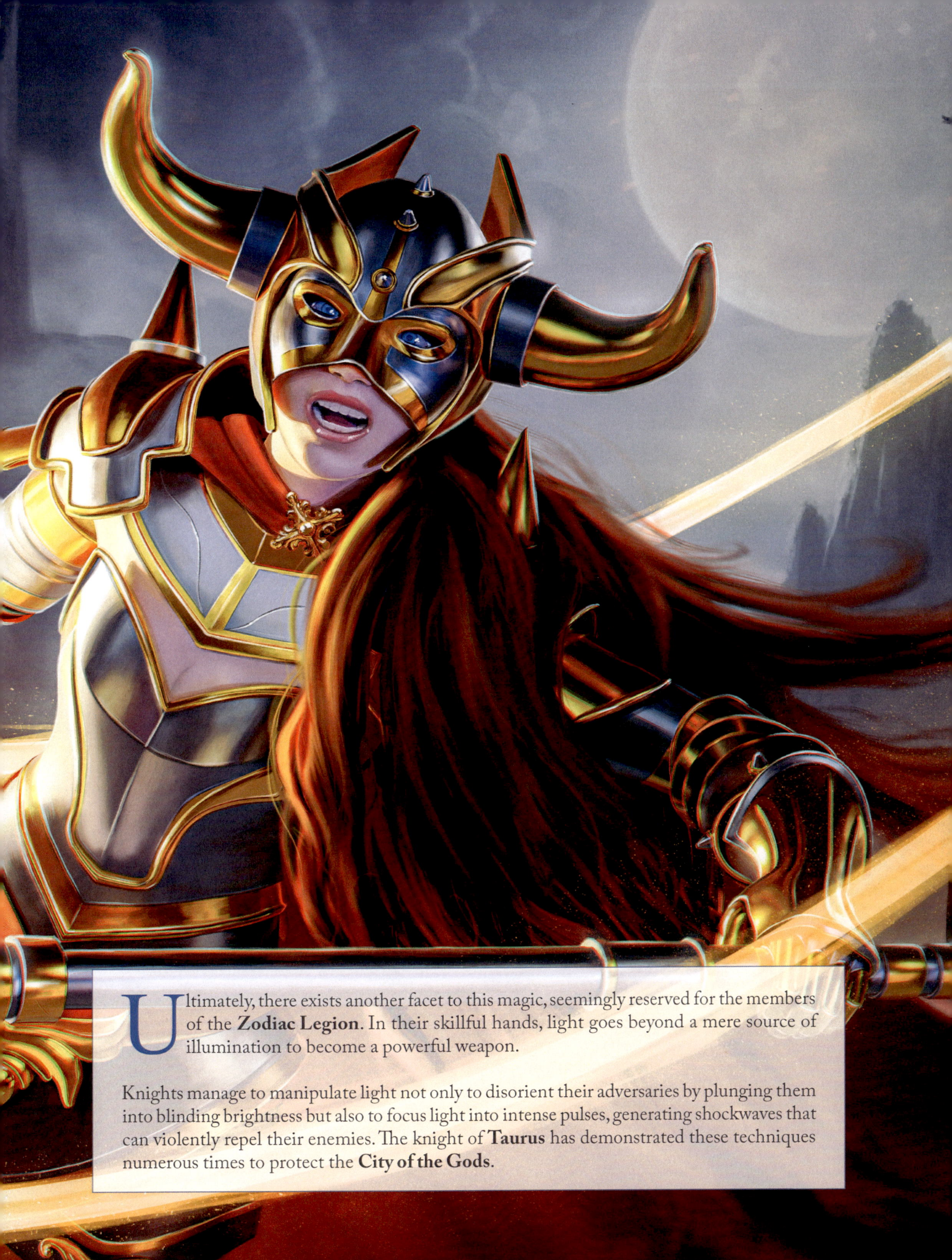

Ultimately, there exists another facet to this magic, seemingly reserved for the members of the **Zodiac Legion**. In their skillful hands, light goes beyond a mere source of illumination to become a powerful weapon.

Knights manage to manipulate light not only to disorient their adversaries by plunging them into blinding brightness but also to focus light into intense pulses, generating shockwaves that can violently repel their enemies. The knight of **Taurus** has demonstrated these techniques numerous times to protect the **City of the Gods**.

DEATH

Death magic is a complex art, almost exclusively under the dominion of the knight of **Cancer**. It is not, strictly speaking, a craft to be practiced but a subject to be studied, as the **Legion** forbids its active use.

Nevertheless, some individuals, known as *"death guards"* or *"guardians of death,"* possess an innate ability to cross the veil separating our world from that of the departed. The **Legion** tolerates this exception, as it extends a measure of solace to grieving families.

This subtle exemption to the rule has allowed specialized researchers to unearth numerous, at times bewildering, discoveries.

The study of this arcane is more akin to an investigative pursuit than a mastery of magic. The death guards, acting instinctively, cannot truly explain their connection. Nevertheless, their testimonies are a valuable source for describing the afterlife and, consequently, shedding light on the nature of our universe.

Critics may rightly question the veracity of the results, dismissing them as mere anecdotal narratives. Yet, it's challenging to disregard the coherence and consistency across different accounts, lending these narratives a degree of credibility.

A notable discovery concerns the existence of an entity named **Hades**, seemingly reigning over the realm of the deceased and overseeing the fate of souls. If you inquire about this with your professors, few will likely venture a definitive opinion on **Hades**' true nature. Nevertheless, it seems plausible that he is indeed one of the gods of **Illuminaria**.

Our understanding of his role remains limited, mainly due to the fragmentary nature of the gathered information. For example, some death guards mention having seen **Hades** "elevate" souls, transforming them into rays of light. But what is the purpose of this act? Is it a judgment of our past lives? Faced with these questions, the knight of **Cancer** merely emphasizes that death is not a punitive measure but rather a quest for perfection.

The onus falls upon us, then, to draw our own conclusions…

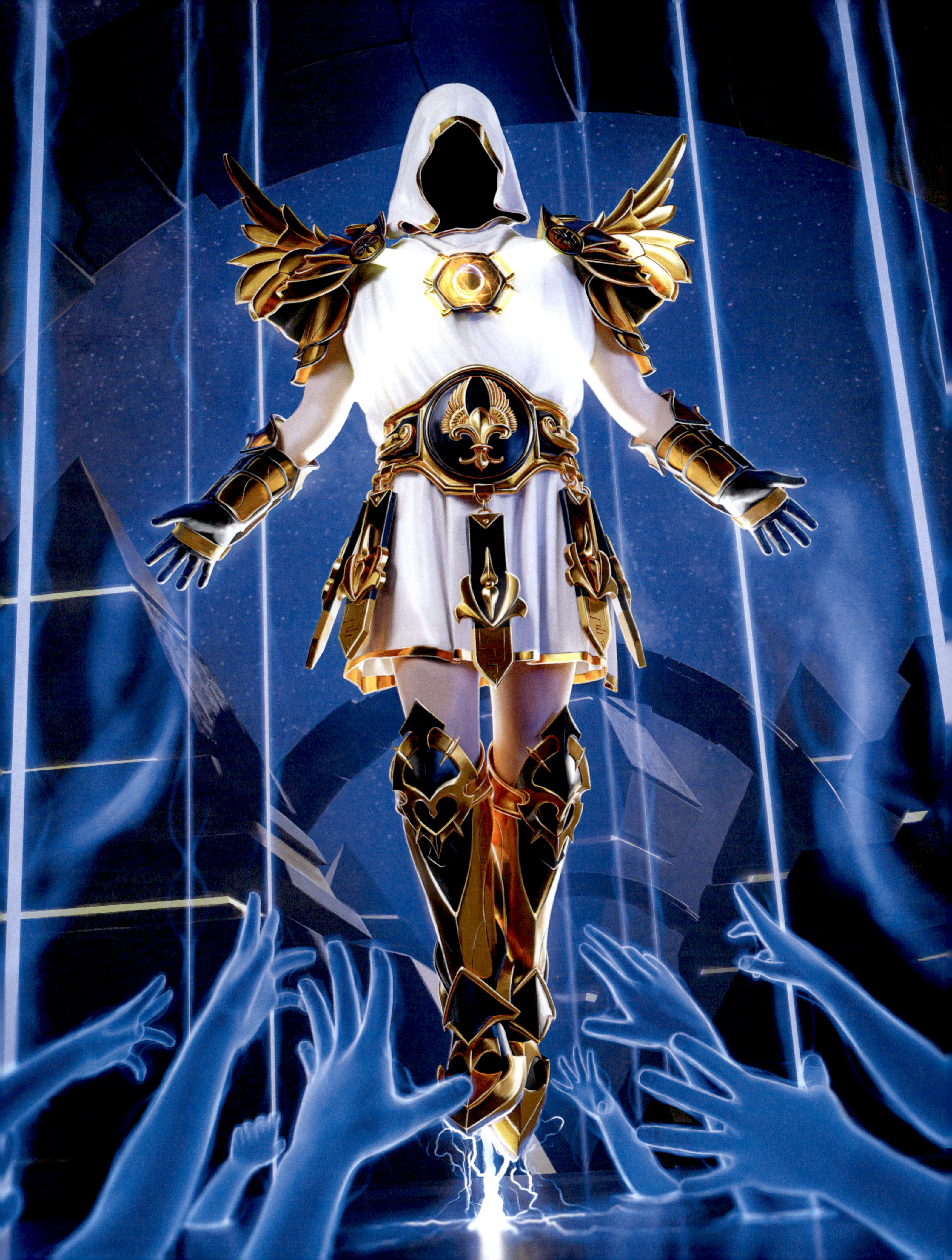

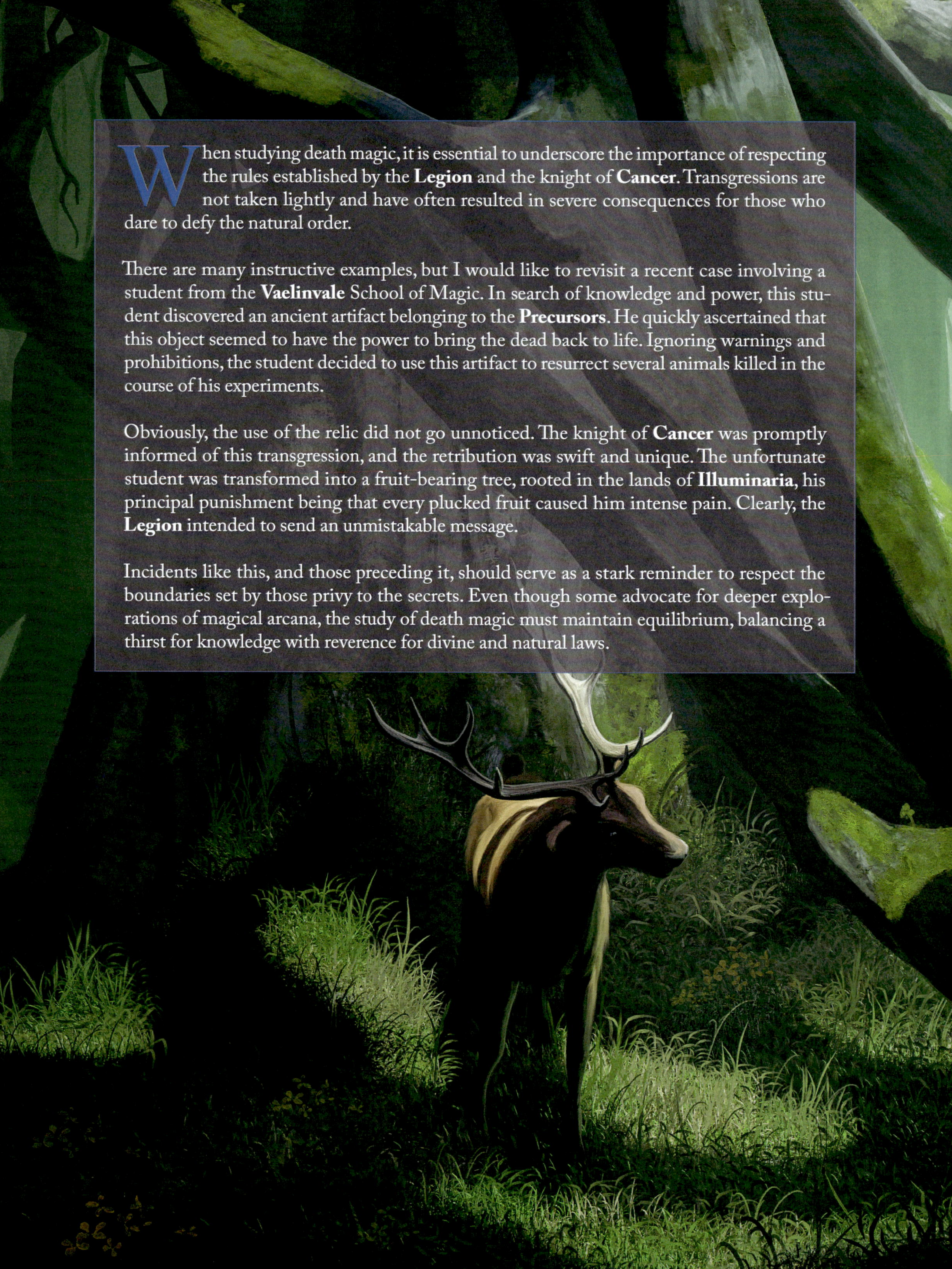

When studying death magic, it is essential to underscore the importance of respecting the rules established by the **Legion** and the knight of **Cancer**. Transgressions are not taken lightly and have often resulted in severe consequences for those who dare to defy the natural order.

There are many instructive examples, but I would like to revisit a recent case involving a student from the **Vaelinvale** School of Magic. In search of knowledge and power, this student discovered an ancient artifact belonging to the **Precursors**. He quickly ascertained that this object seemed to have the power to bring the dead back to life. Ignoring warnings and prohibitions, the student decided to use this artifact to resurrect several animals killed in the course of his experiments.

Obviously, the use of the relic did not go unnoticed. The knight of **Cancer** was promptly informed of this transgression, and the retribution was swift and unique. The unfortunate student was transformed into a fruit-bearing tree, rooted in the lands of **Illuminaria**, his principal punishment being that every plucked fruit caused him intense pain. Clearly, the **Legion** intended to send an unmistakable message.

Incidents like this, and those preceding it, should serve as a stark reminder to respect the boundaries set by those privy to the secrets. Even though some advocate for deeper explorations of magical arcana, the study of death magic must maintain equilibrium, balancing a thirst for knowledge with reverence for divine and natural laws.

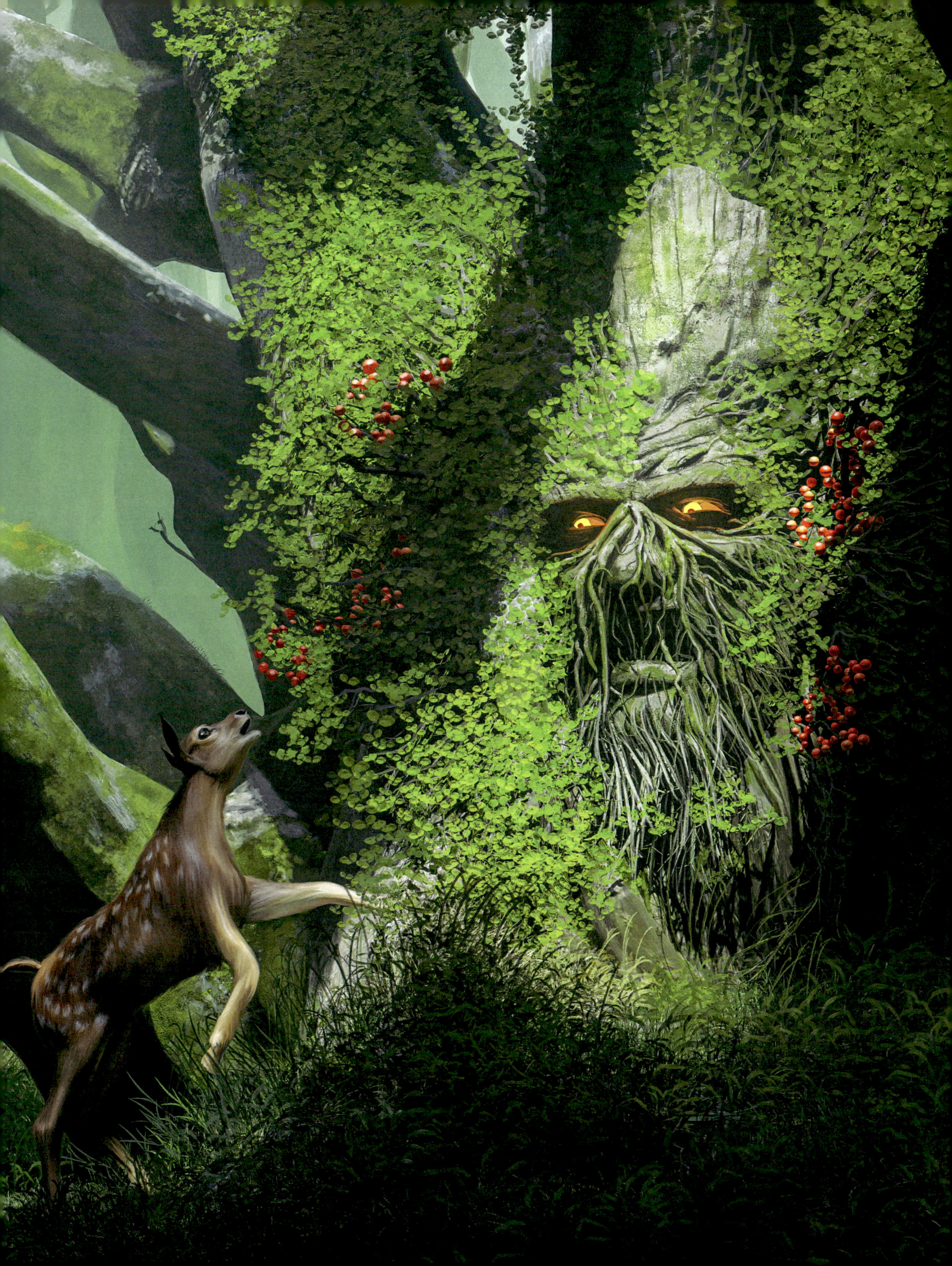

NATURE

The magic of nature stands as the bedrock of **Illuminaria's** equilibrium, surpassing the mere ability to nurture a plant or converse with an animal. It is a communion with life itself, the vibrant and ever-changing fabric that constitutes our world.

Masters of this magic can not only communicate with animals but also guide the growth of plants. In regions where wild animals pose challenges, nature mages are invaluable. They pacify beasts, avert conflicts, and provide mounts and draft animals.

Similarly, during challenging seasons when crops are threatened, their ability to encourage plant growth is invaluable. They mitigate the impact of poor harvests and offer hope in times of darkness.

However, nature magic is also shrouded in a veil of mystery. Persistent rumors speak of a mystical presence associated with this magic. Many farmers claim to have witnessed a figure clad in golden armor, walking through their fields alongside three great wolves. This apparition seems more frequent after natural disasters, such as wildfires or earthquakes. Testimonies converge on one idea: this entity supports nature in its healing, aiding forests in rebirth and lands in regaining fertility. When questioned on the matter, the knight of **Pisces** remains elusive about the nature of this character.

Nevertheless, a scholar from the **Great Library** recently made a disconcerting discovery. While exploring ancient manuscripts, he stumbled upon multiple references to an entity named **Demeter**. The texts suggest that **Demeter** is linked to the ecosystem of **Illuminaria**. Several theories circulate, with one gaining particular attention: **Demeter** could well be an ancient goddess, overseeing nature and ensuring the continuity of life on **Illuminaria**.

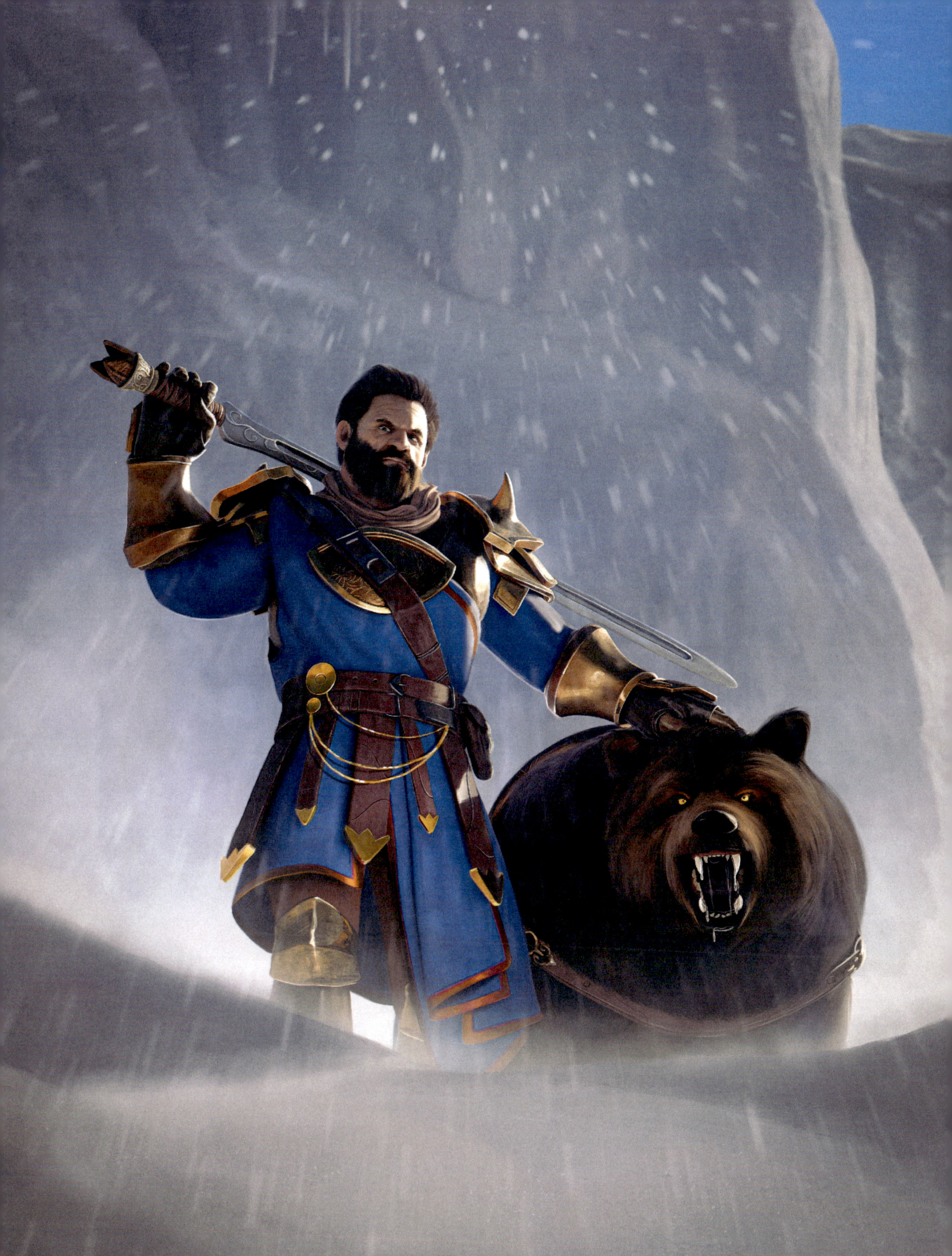

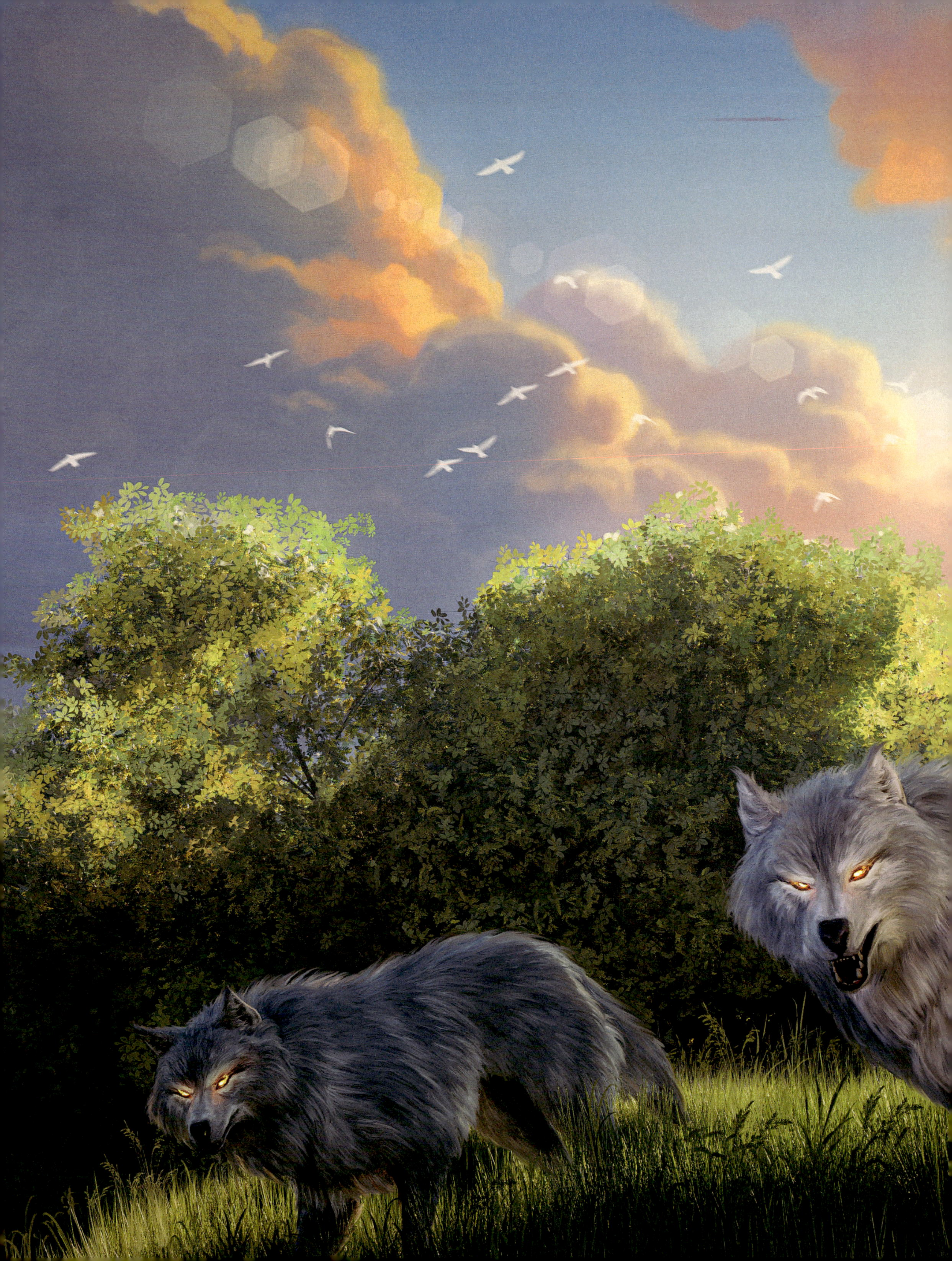

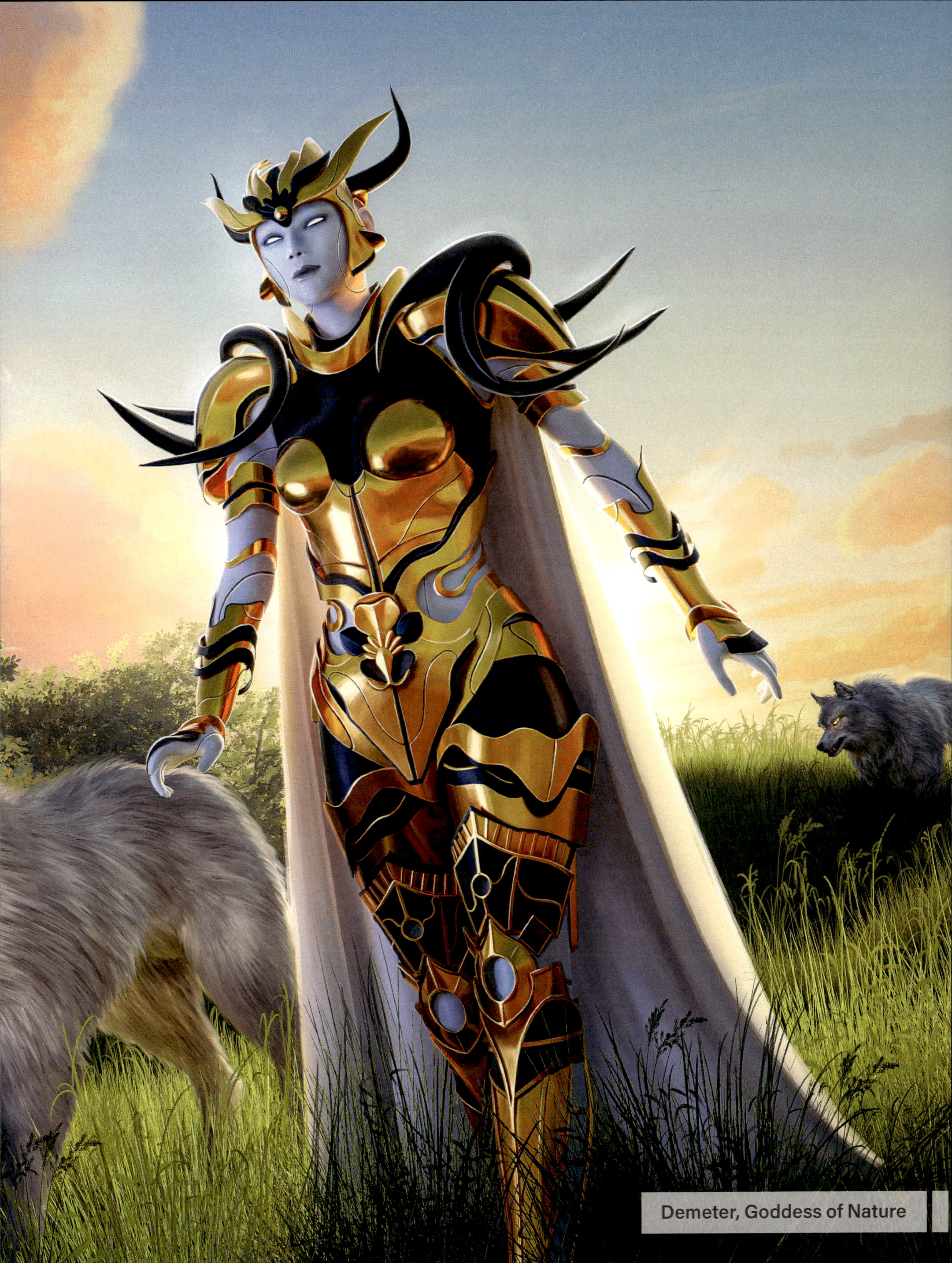

Demeter, Goddess of Nature

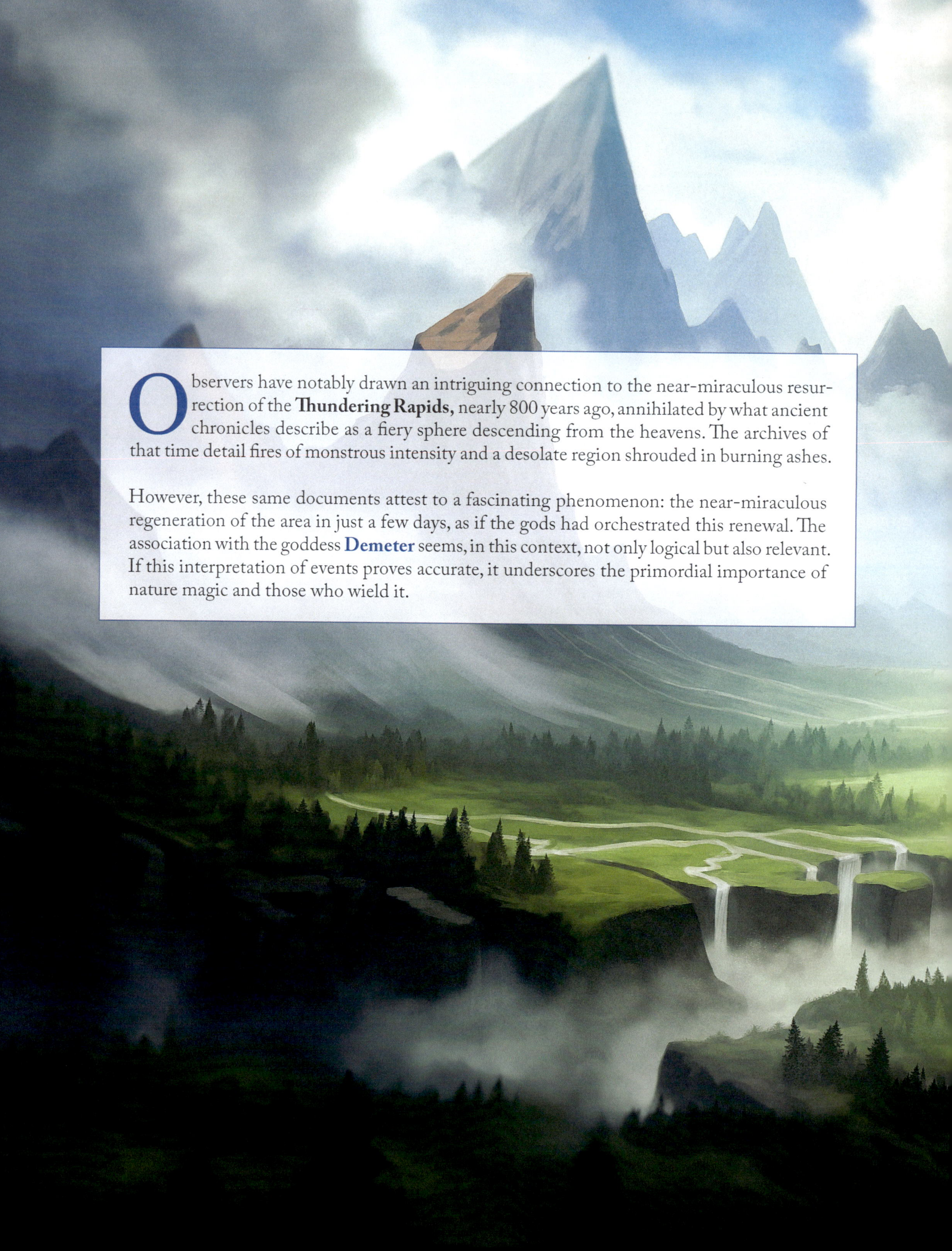

Observers have notably drawn an intriguing connection to the near-miraculous resurrection of the **Thundering Rapids,** nearly 800 years ago, annihilated by what ancient chronicles describe as a fiery sphere descending from the heavens. The archives of that time detail fires of monstrous intensity and a desolate region shrouded in burning ashes.

However, these same documents attest to a fascinating phenomenon: the near-miraculous regeneration of the area in just a few days, as if the gods had orchestrated this renewal. The association with the goddess **Demeter** seems, in this context, not only logical but also relevant. If this interpretation of events proves accurate, it underscores the primordial importance of nature magic and those who wield it.

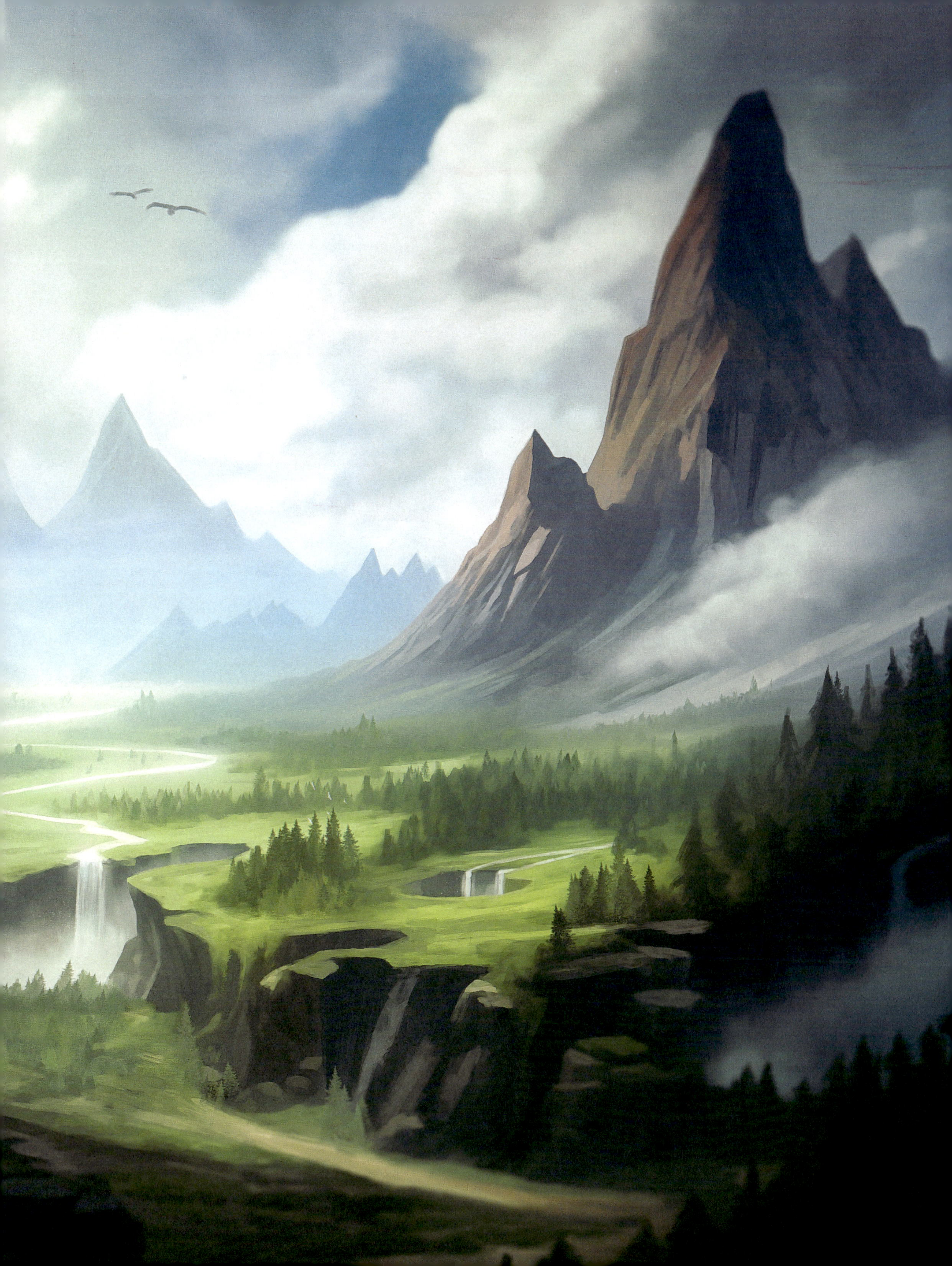

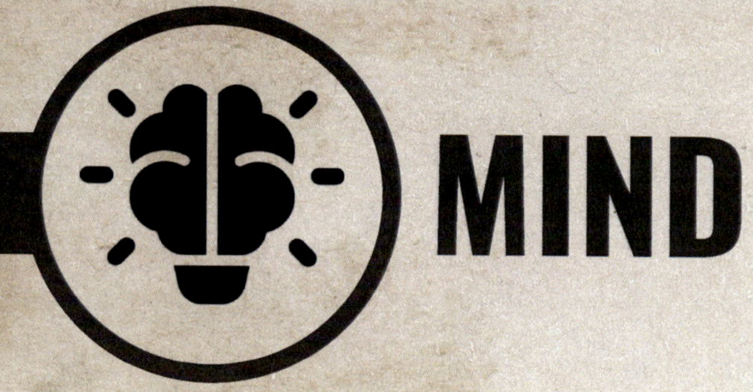

MIND

A mong **Illuminaria's** most mysterious arcana, spirit magic undeniably claims a prime spot. Currently beyond our capability to harness, it is nonetheless acknowledged for its existence.

How? Because it's the magic employed by the two Spirit Stones.

These were discovered 50 years ago during excavations in the ruins of the ancient city (often referred to as the **Metal City**) located south of **Kosh**.

The first, named **Cataclysm**, is an amber stone partially embedded in a block of volcanic rock. The slightest contact with its surface projects a message of startling realism into your mind, as if a voice were whispering in your ear. Only the person in contact with the stone can hear this message.

The transcribed message below revolutionized our worldview, as it seems the voice we hear through the stone was emitted by a **Precursor**:

"My name is Aska Moriviani, and I'm using my last memory stone to record this message. A cataclysm has just occurred, and I don't know what will become of me. Everyone around me is dead. They were all shot without being able to react. I've been wandering for days in an empty city. No networks work anymore; I can't connect to any data clusters."

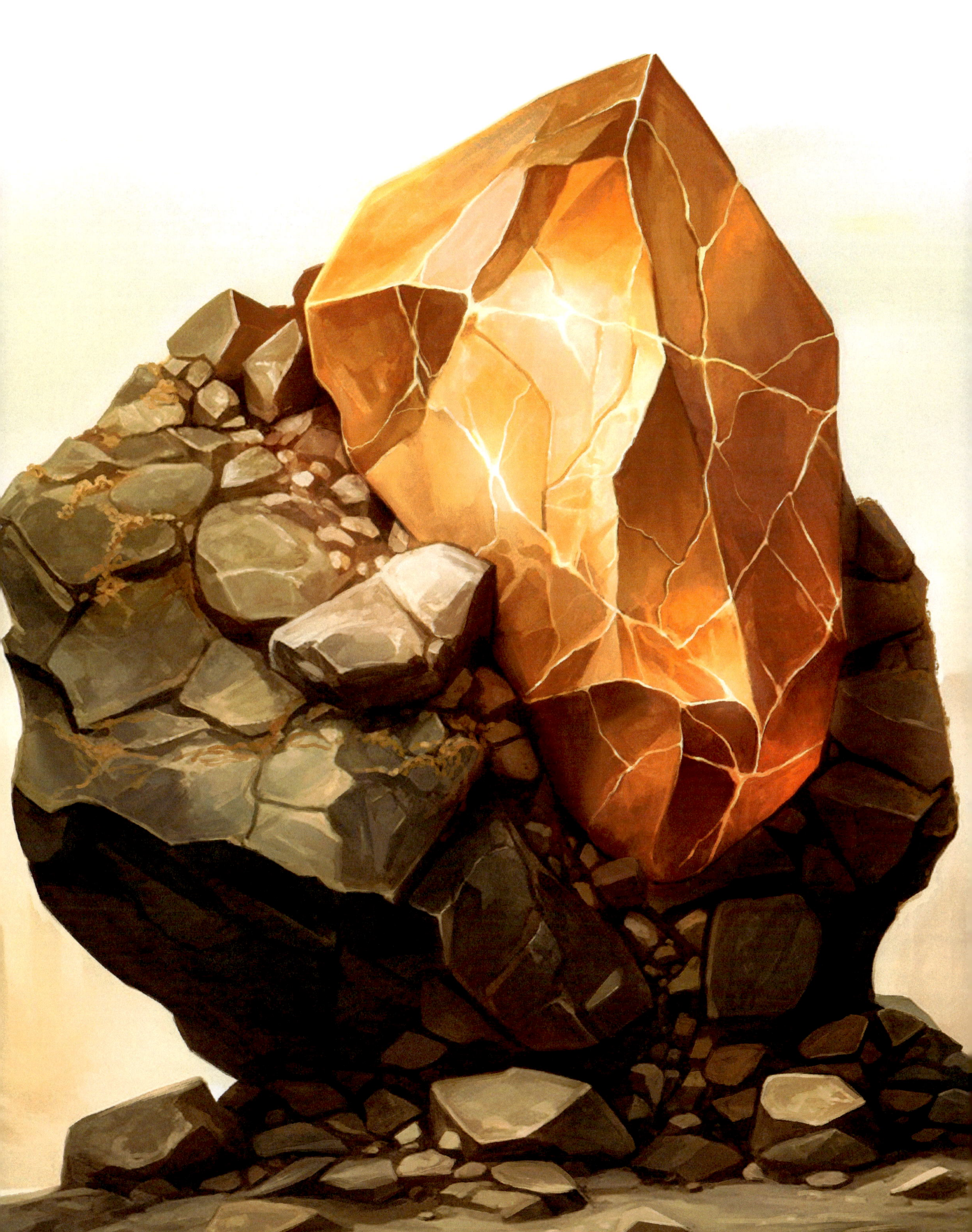

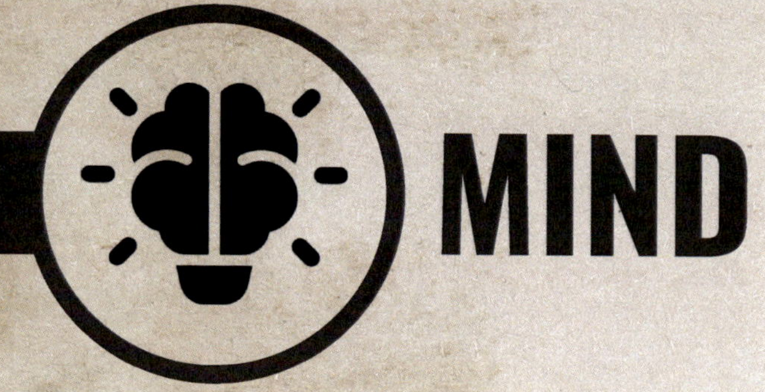

MIND

The second stone, named **Despair**, is composed of an emerald set in a concretion and also contains a message, but seemingly not from the same person:

"I just woke up from my operation, alone, still connected to the regenerative capacitors. Everyone is dead! I don't understand what happened! Oh, by all the saints! Zeus's ultimatum! It can only be that! He warned us. What horror! What will become of me? Nothing works anymore. Only the memory stones still seem to accept connection requests."

As you can see, we're dealing with a potent magic that communicates directly into our minds. Unfortunately, all our attempts to reproduce the phenomenon and establish a telepathic link between two people have thus far failed.

These two messages (of which our understanding of the content is unfortunately limited) are still today the only manifestations of this powerful arcane, as well as the only testimonies related to the history of the **Precursors**. Indeed, all excavations in the ruins of their civilization have never yielded anything tangible.

The current theory thus indicates that an entity named **Zeus** would have eradicated their entire civilization, leaving only a few people alive and freezing their civilization forever.

Who is this **Zeus**? On this subject, the **Legion** remains silent, and the **Great Library** contains no references associated with this name. Naturally, many believe that **Zeus** could be a god of **Illuminaria** who was deeply angered by the **Precursors** for reasons still unknown.

It is therefore our duty to continue studying spirit magic, hoping that it may one day open the doors to our past.

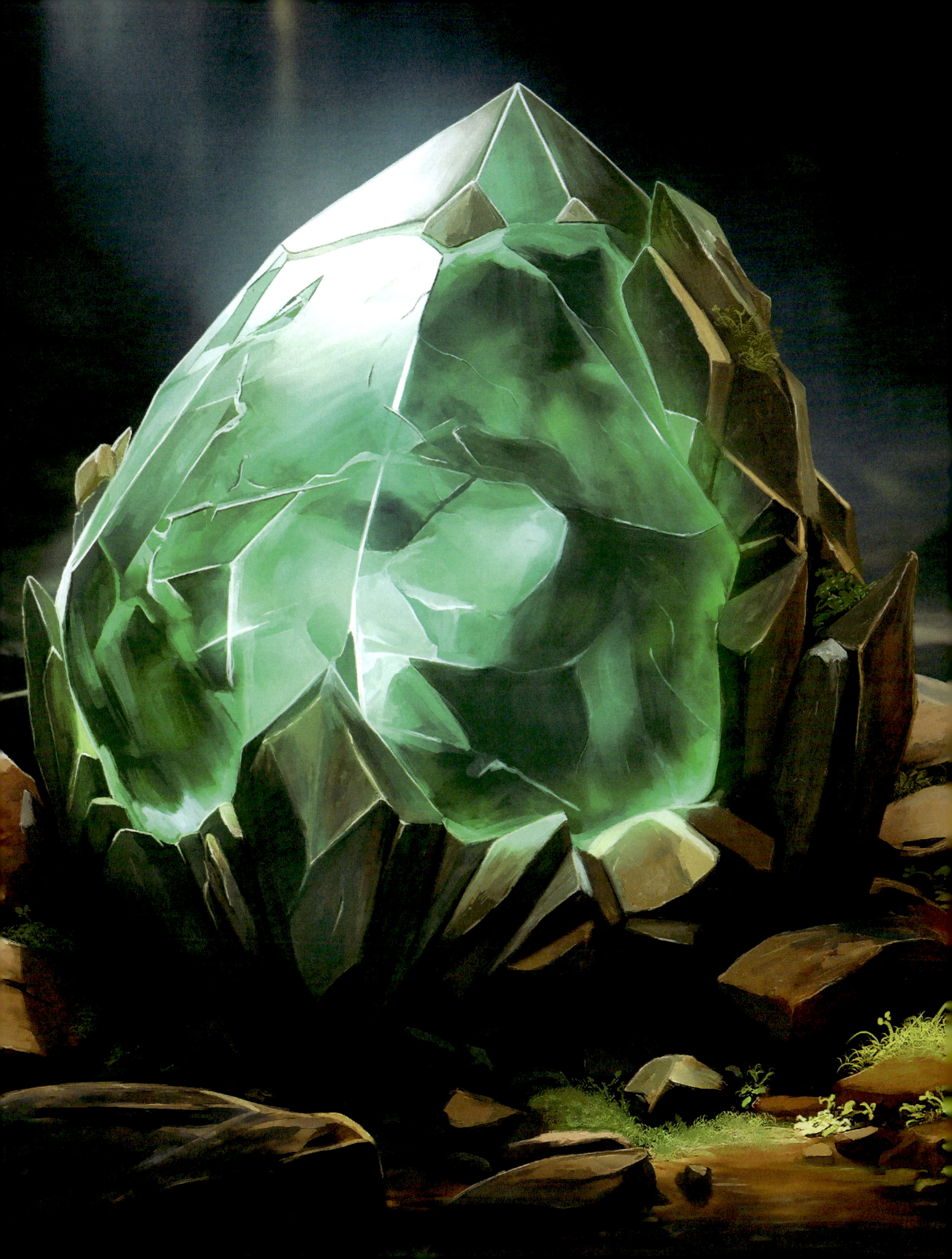

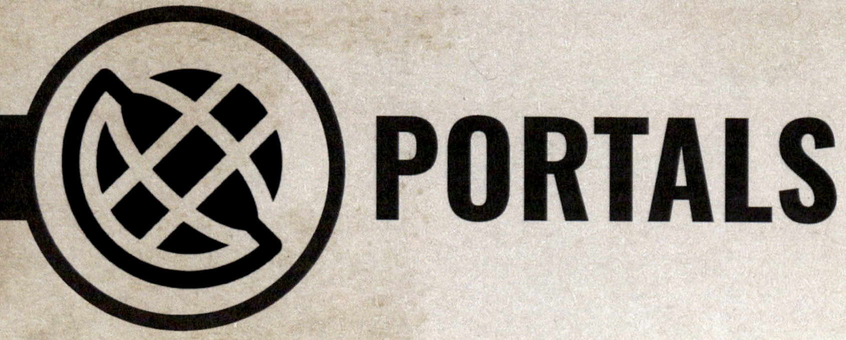

PORTALS

In the vast spectrum of magical arts in **Illuminaria**, portal magic remains highly mysterious. Its operation, origin, and true nature completely elude us. What makes it even more intriguing is our total inability to even scratch the surface of this magic. While other magical domains have been tamed or at least understood to some extent, portal magic retains its persistent enigmatic allure.

As far back as memory serves, these structures have always existed. Shaped like a semicircle of stone, portals open a passage for instantaneous and seamless movement between extremely distant locations. It's not a phenomenon that can be simply ignored, given its enormous potential utility.

Invariably, each of these portals is found near one or more mana pyramids. It seems logical to consider that the phenomenal amount of mana needed to create a rift in space would be directly drawn from these pyramids, but the truth of this hypothesis remains to be demonstrated.

Too many questions linger. Who built these portals? Are they the work of gods, the **Precursors**, or a now-forgotten civilization? Interestingly, although the **Legion** is known for its incredible feats and vast knowledge, no reference or mention of it having the ability to open a portal has ever been found.

Portal magic, despite the mysteries surrounding it, remains an extremely active field of research. Mastery of instantaneous travel would open unimaginable prospects for humankind. Whether for exploration, trade, or even diplomacy, the power to move without the constraints of distance would transform **Illuminaria** forever.

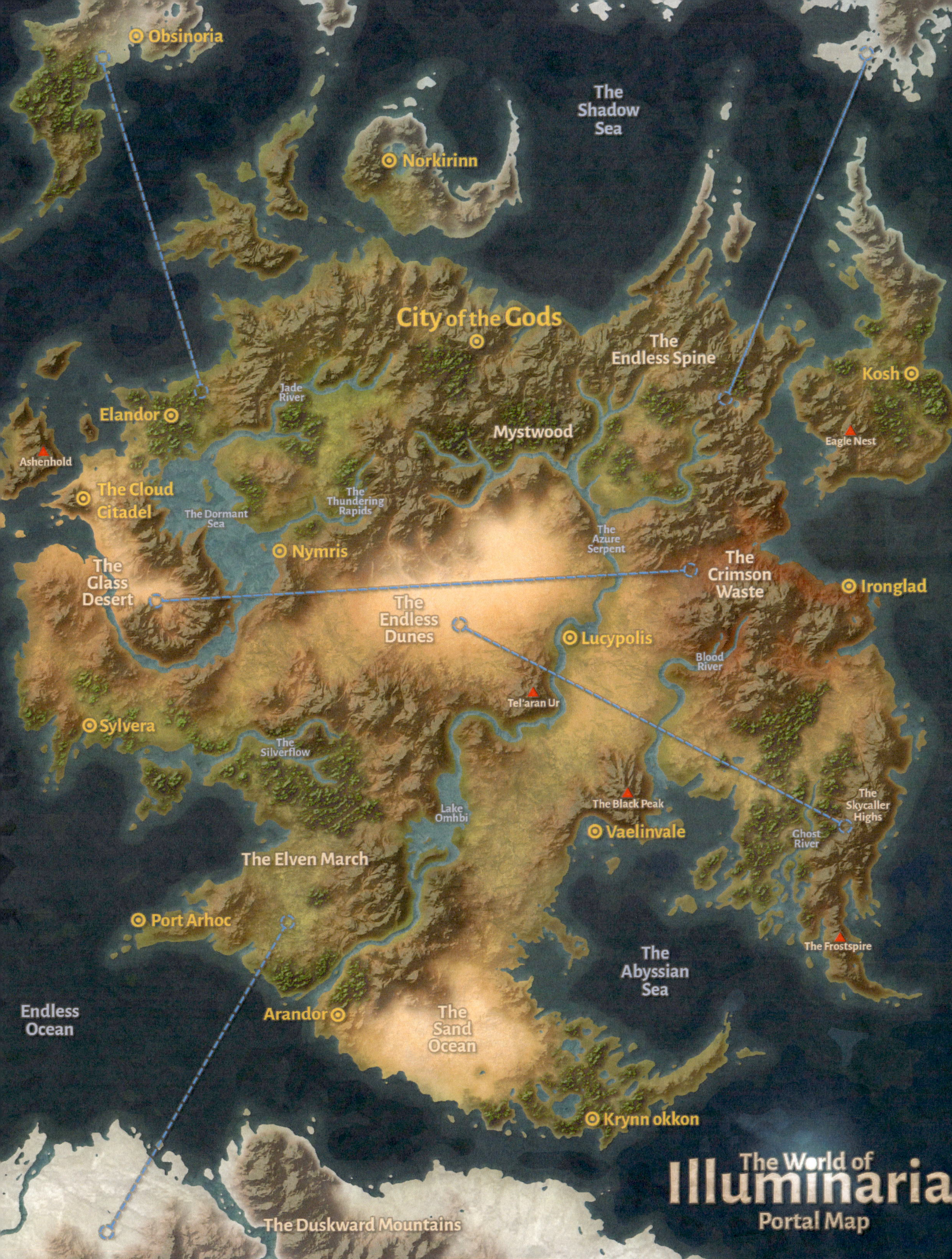

Obsinoria
Norkirinn
The Shadow Sea
Kosh
City of the Gods
The Endless Spine
Jade River
Elandor
Eagle Nest
Ashenhold
Mystwood
The Cloud Citadel
The Dormant Sea
The Thundering Rapids
The Azure Serpent
Nymris
The Crimson Waste
Ironglad
The Glass Desert
The Endless Dunes
Lucypolis
Blood River
Sylvera
Tel'aran Ur
The Silverflow
Lake Omhbi
The Black Peak
The Skycaller Highs
The Elven March
Vaelinvale
Ghost River
Port Arhoc
The Frostspire
Endless Ocean
Arandor
The Sand Ocean
The Abyssian Sea
Krynn okkon
The Duskward Mountains
The World of
Illuminaria
Portal Map

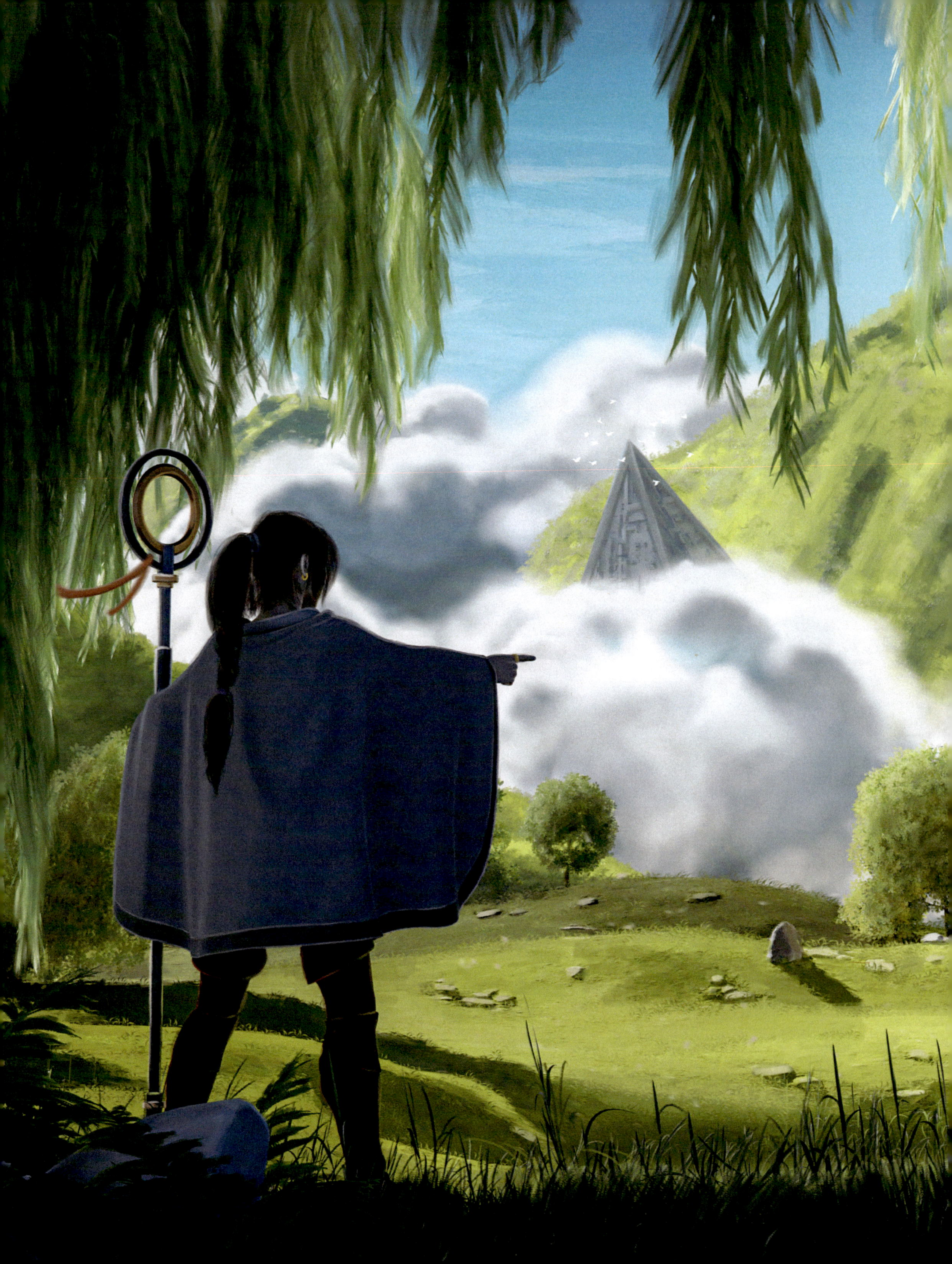

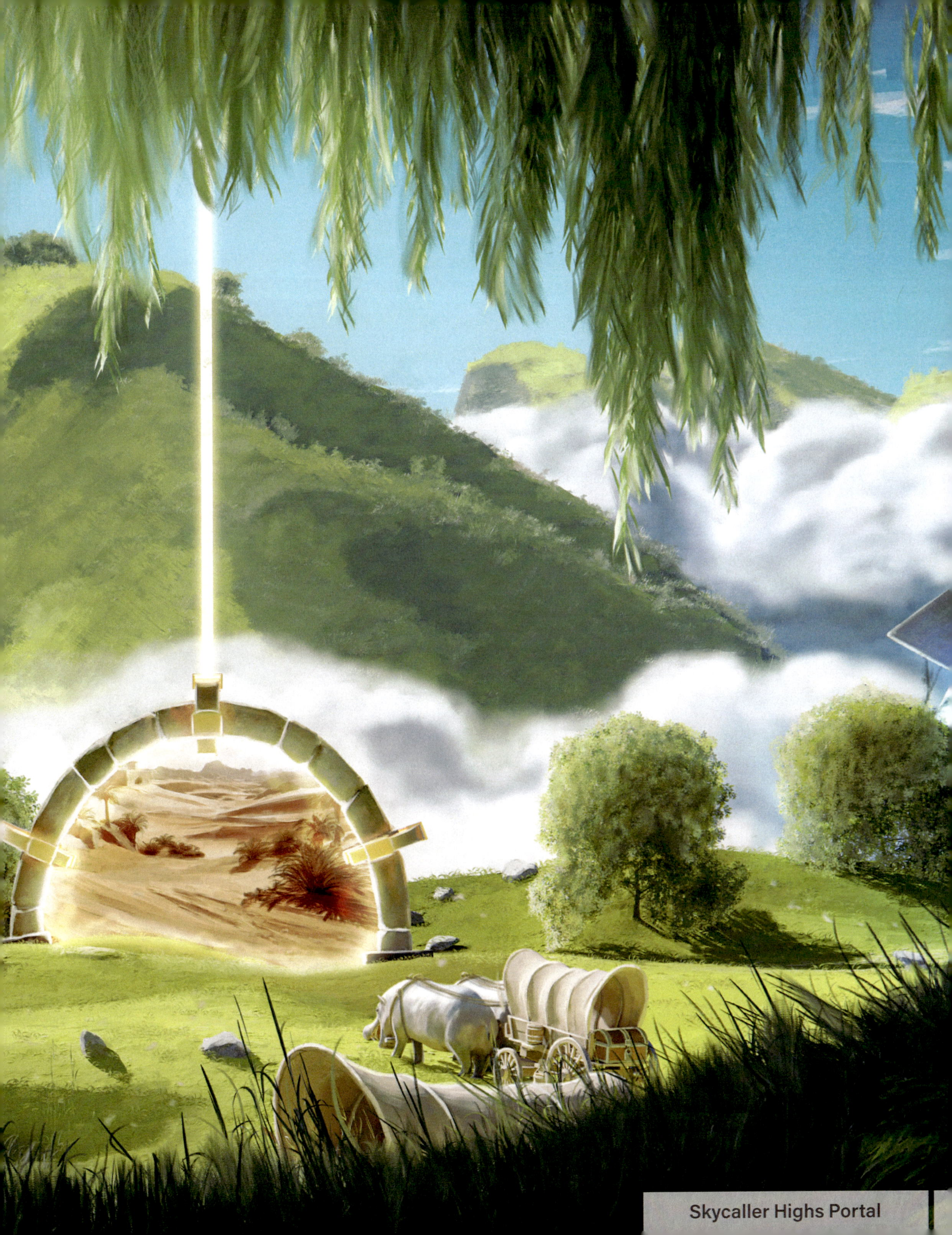

Skycaller Highs Portal

PRECURSOR
MAGIC

There are mysteries that history cherishes, acting as bridges between a bygone past and the promises of the future. The **Precursors** undoubtedly fall into this category. The ruins of their majestic cities stand among **Illuminaria's** most precious archaeological treasures, silent witnesses to a once-thriving civilization.

Despite the inexorable passage of time, these structures stand tall, revealing a level of architectural mastery not known to us today. They showcase pure and harmonious forms, crafted with advanced expertise in metal and unknown materials, as well as magic we still struggle to grasp.

Where our buildings are made of stone and wood, those of the **Precursors** shine with a unique mastery of metallurgy. Artifacts discovered in these ruins, some of which are still operational, suggest a time when magic and metal mastery coexisted, undoubtedly forming the foundation of their daily lives.

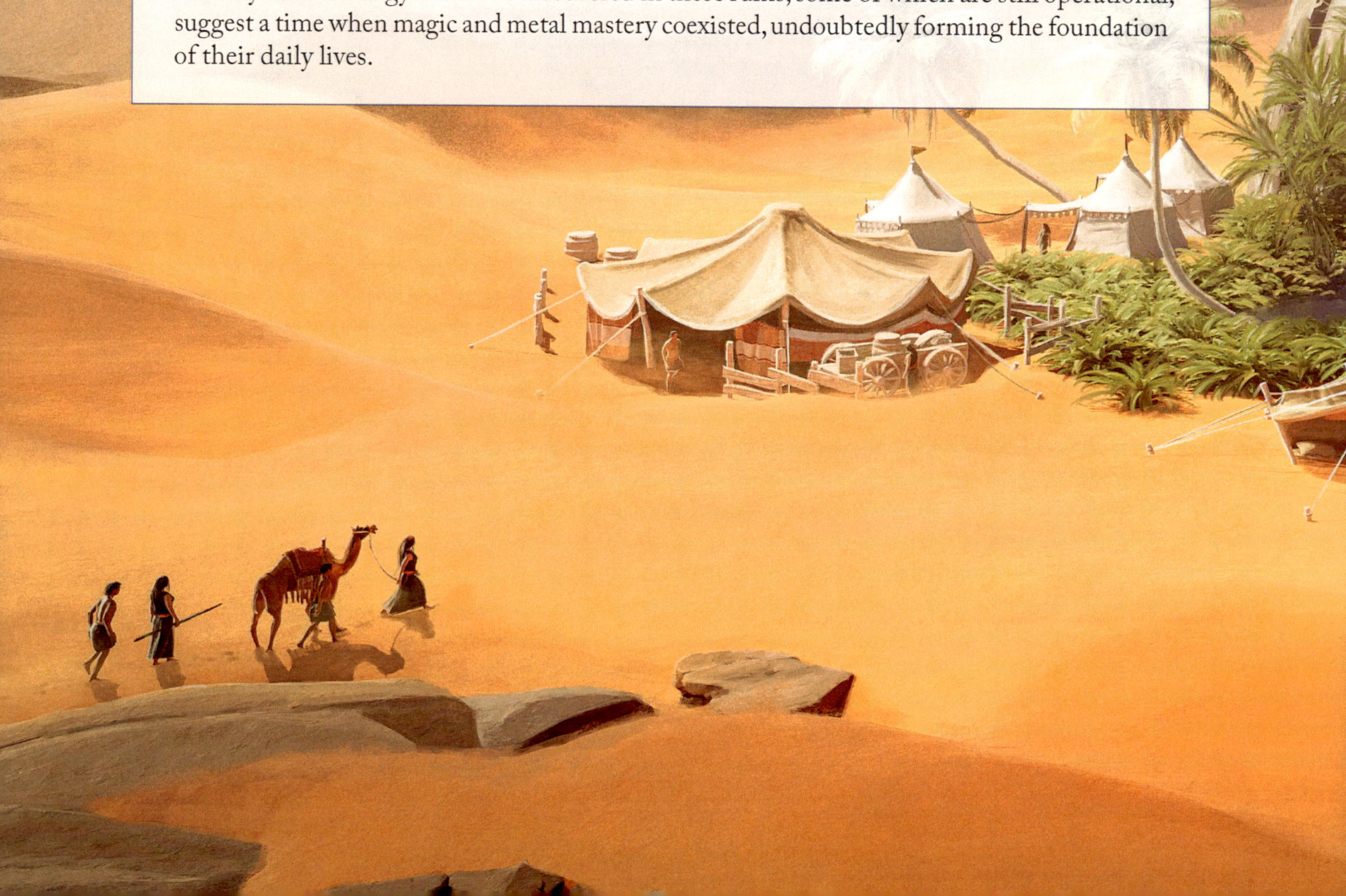

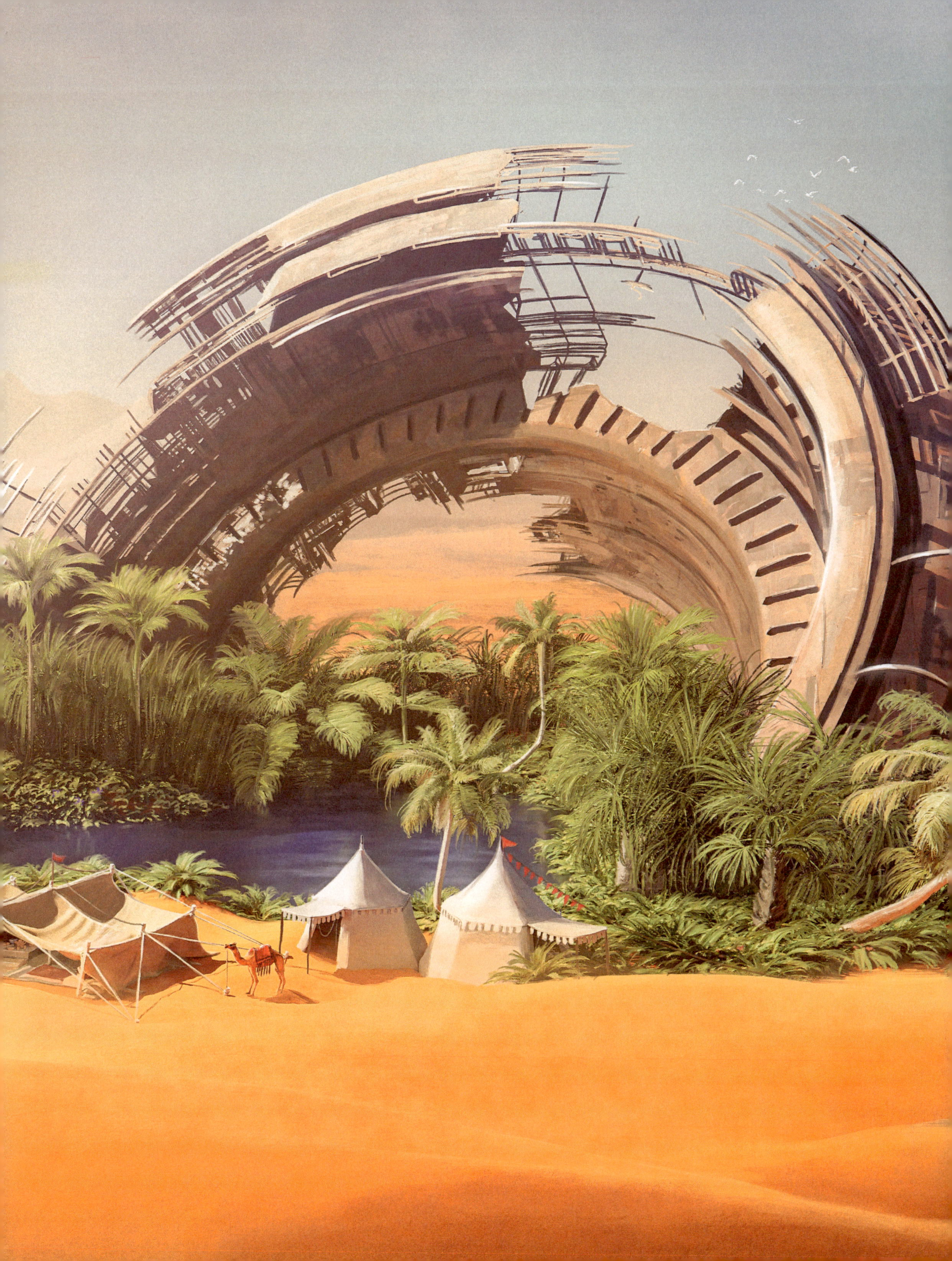

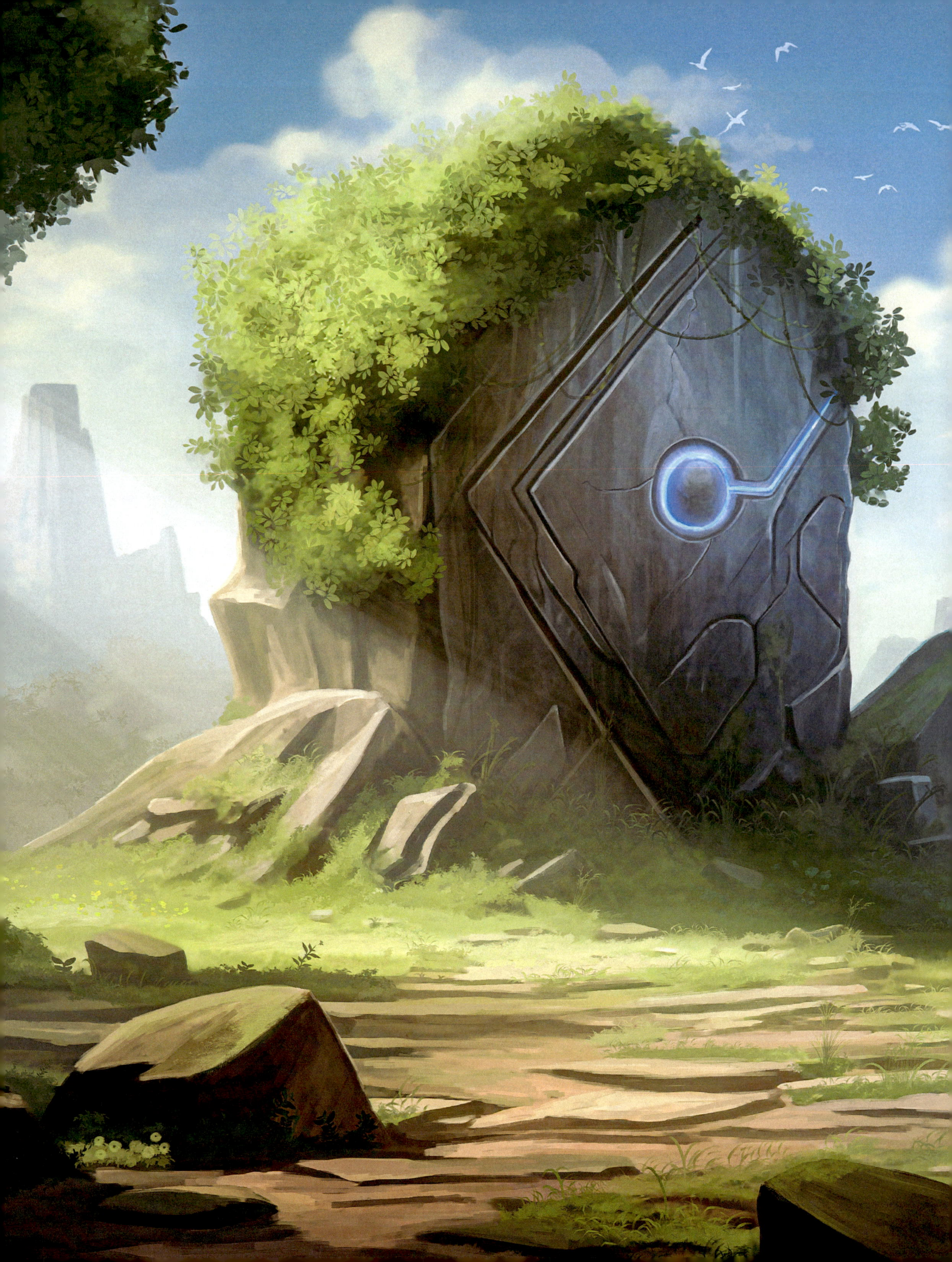

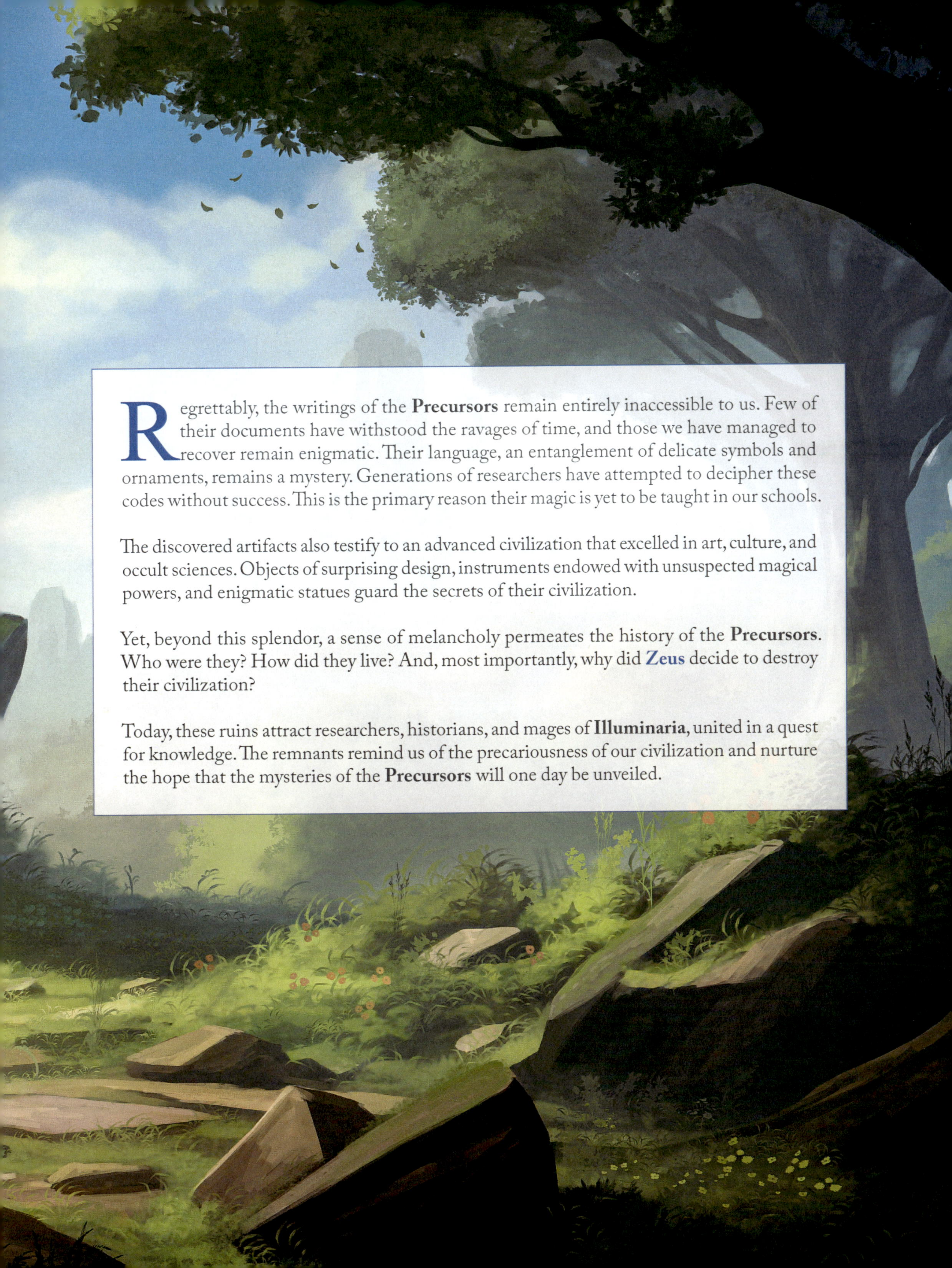

Regrettably, the writings of the **Precursors** remain entirely inaccessible to us. Few of their documents have withstood the ravages of time, and those we have managed to recover remain enigmatic. Their language, an entanglement of delicate symbols and ornaments, remains a mystery. Generations of researchers have attempted to decipher these codes without success. This is the primary reason their magic is yet to be taught in our schools.

The discovered artifacts also testify to an advanced civilization that excelled in art, culture, and occult sciences. Objects of surprising design, instruments endowed with unsuspected magical powers, and enigmatic statues guard the secrets of their civilization.

Yet, beyond this splendor, a sense of melancholy permeates the history of the **Precursors**. Who were they? How did they live? And, most importantly, why did **Zeus** decide to destroy their civilization?

Today, these ruins attract researchers, historians, and mages of **Illuminaria**, united in a quest for knowledge. The remnants remind us of the precariousness of our civilization and nurture the hope that the mysteries of the **Precursors** will one day be unveiled.

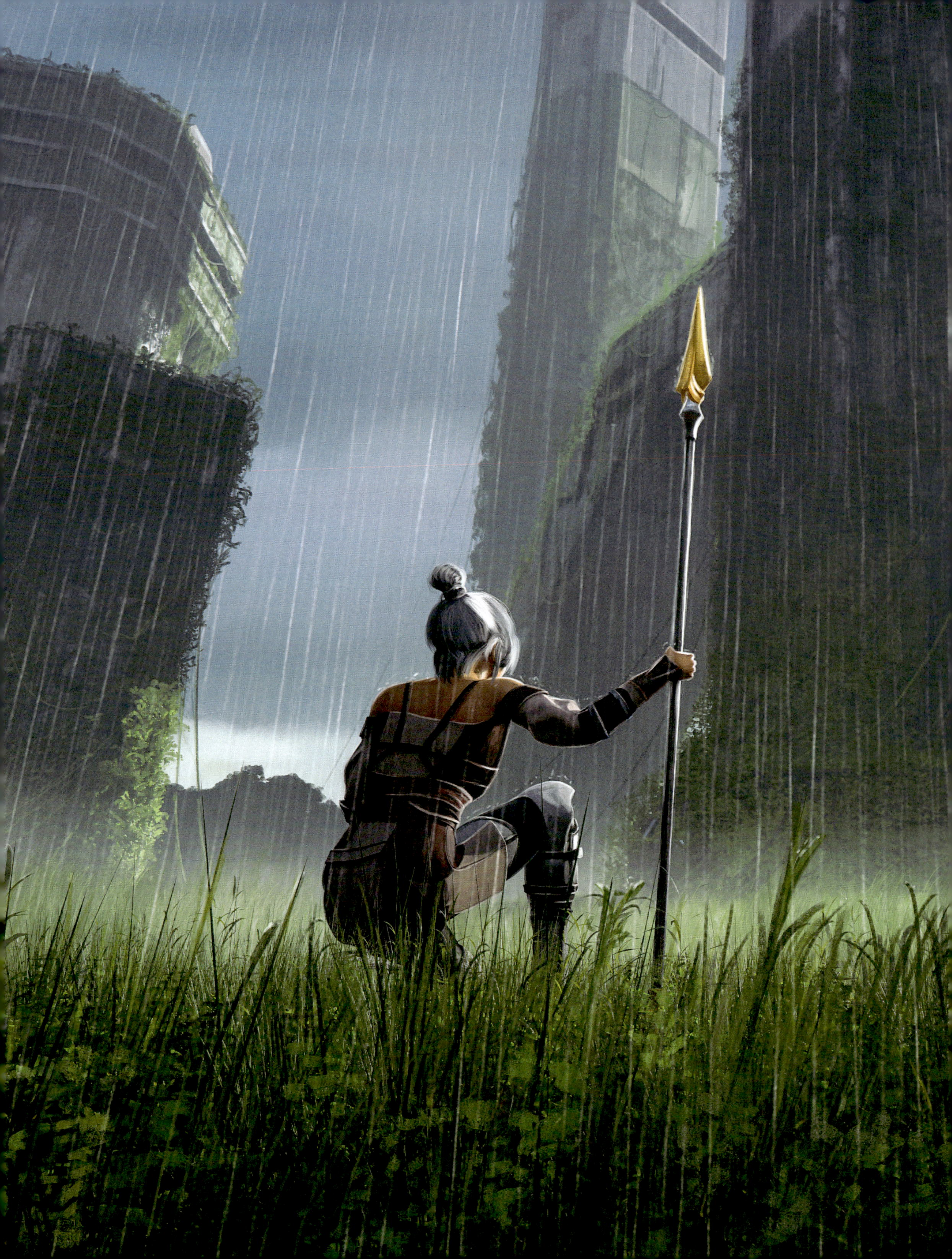

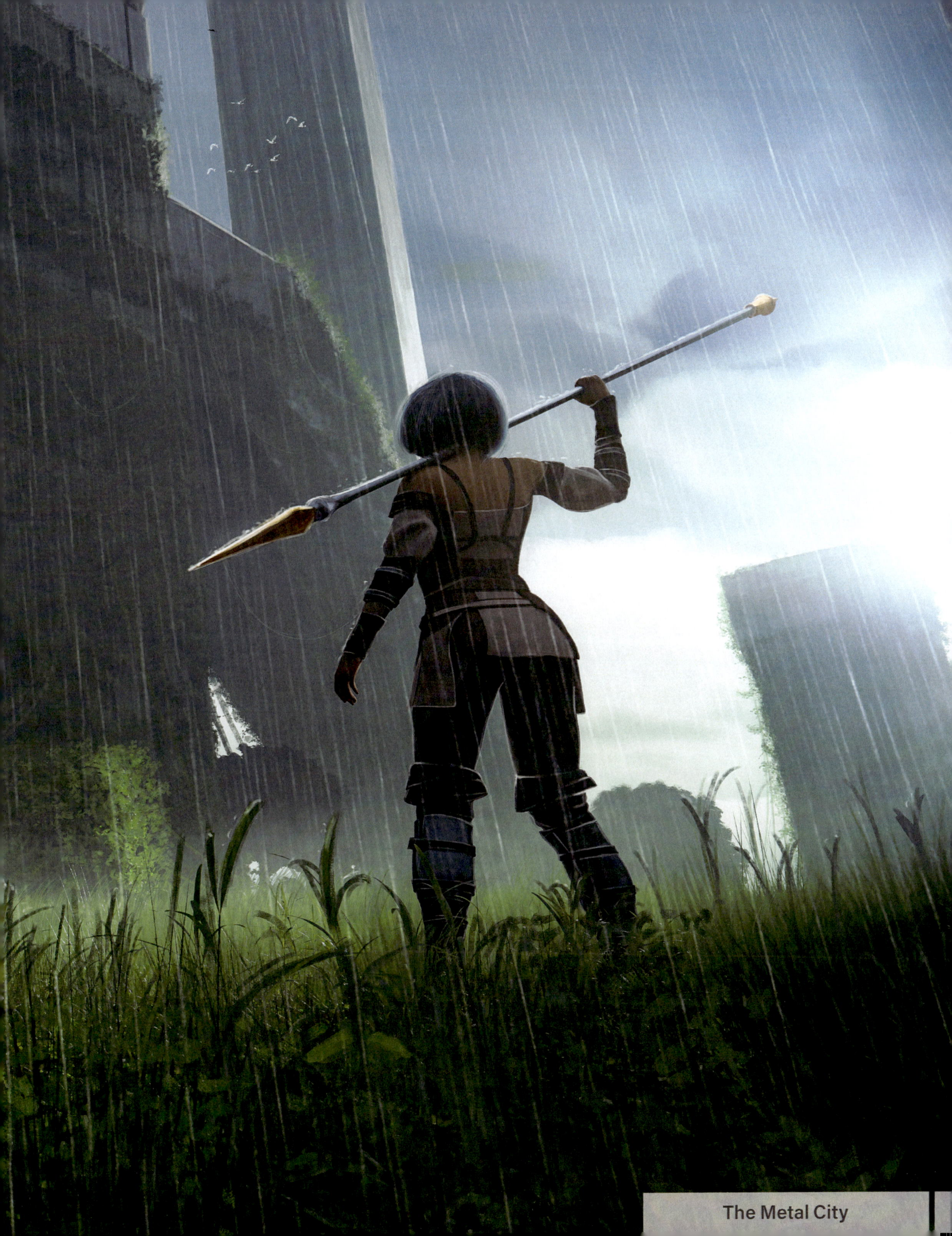

The Metal City

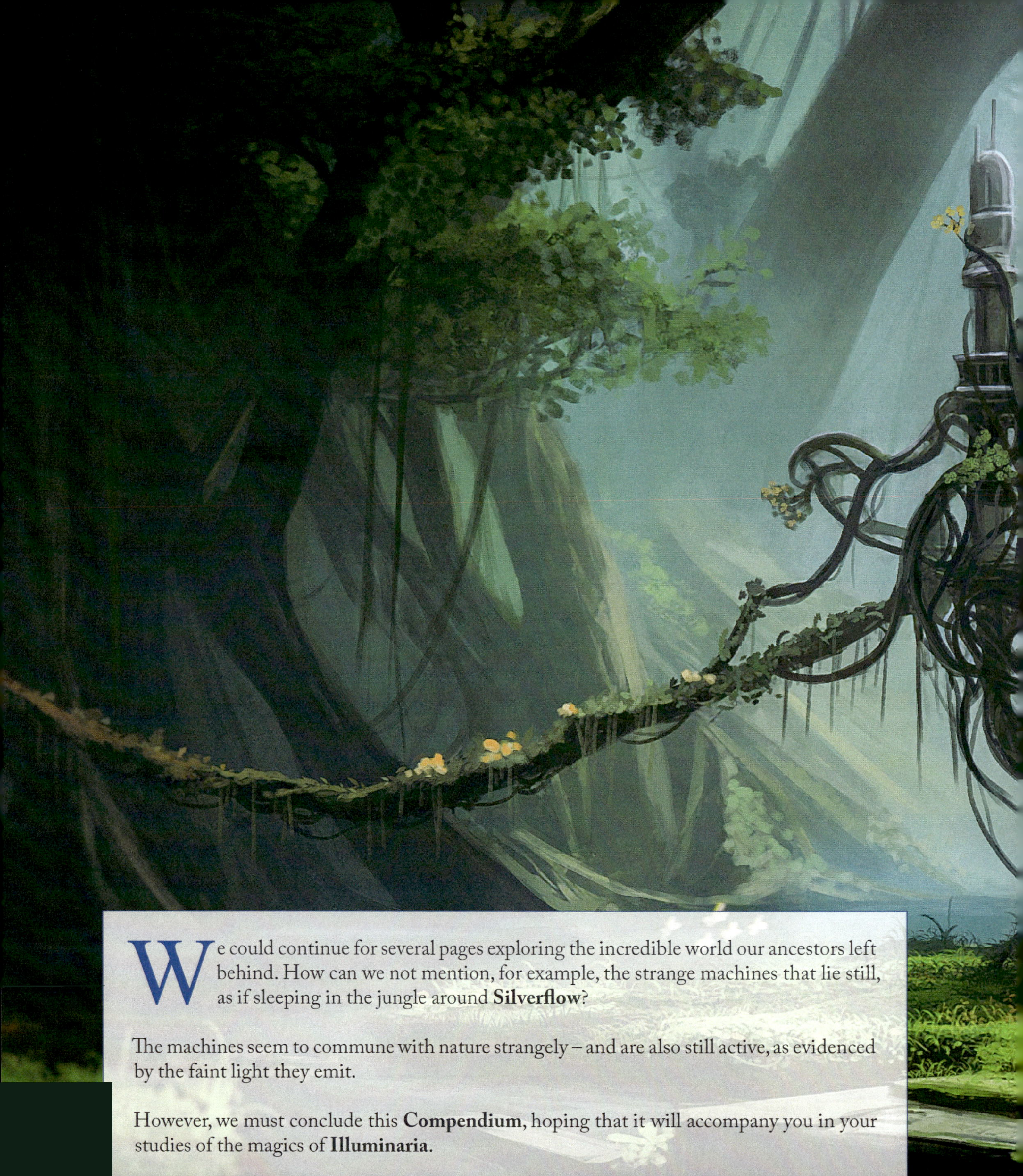

We could continue for several pages exploring the incredible world our ancestors left behind. How can we not mention, for example, the strange machines that lie still, as if sleeping in the jungle around **Silverflow**?

The machines seem to commune with nature strangely – and are also still active, as evidenced by the faint light they emit.

However, we must conclude this **Compendium**, hoping that it will accompany you in your studies of the magics of **Illuminaria**.

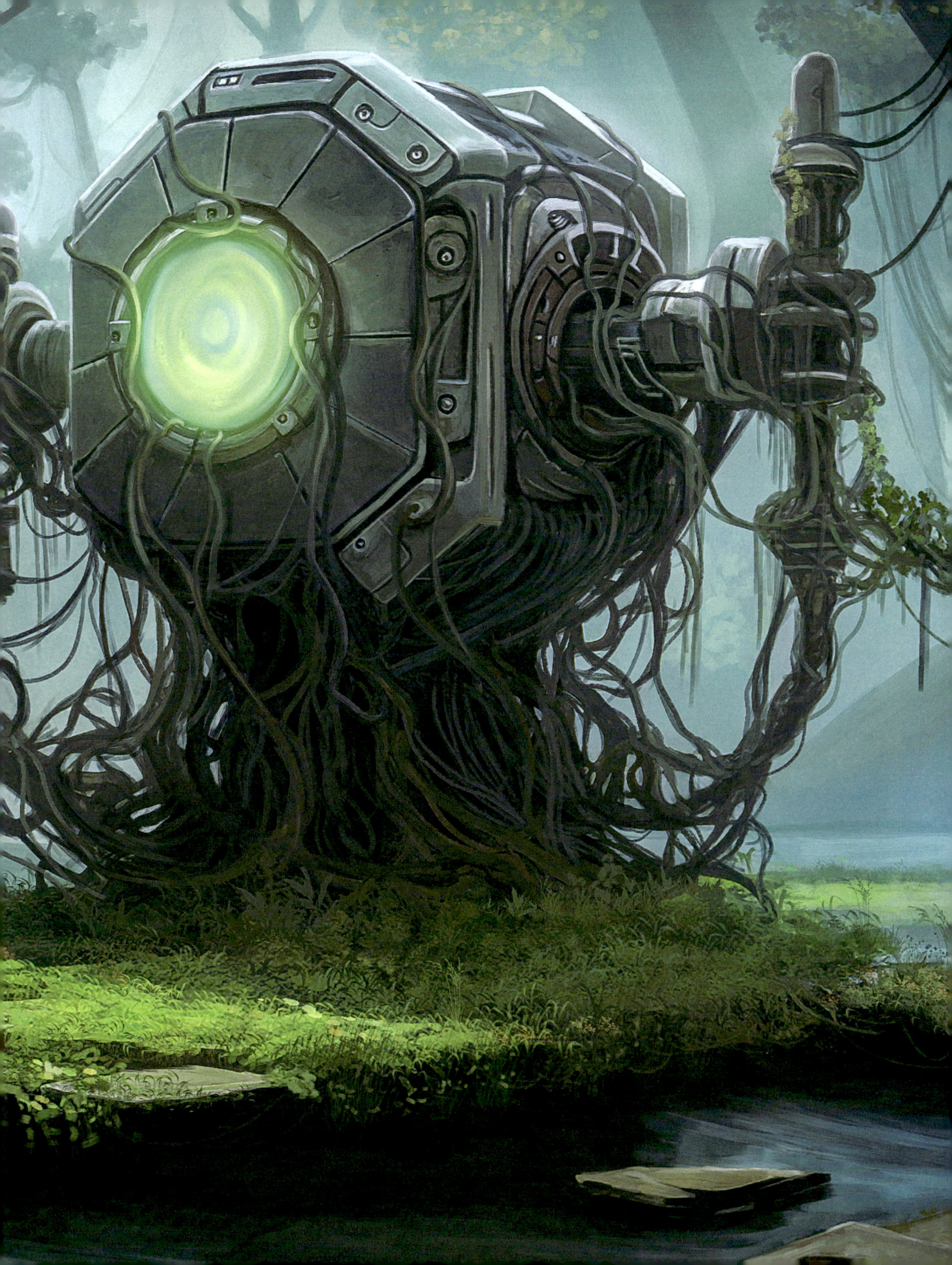

Dear readers,

This second volume owes its existence to your unwavering support, and I trust these tales have sparked as much wonder and fascination in you as they have in me as I write them.

They are the result of several years of gestation before I finally decided to learn to draw to put them on paper. It just goes to show, it's never too late!

May the magic of **Illuminaria** accompany you in your journeys!

With all my gratitude,
Deltakosh

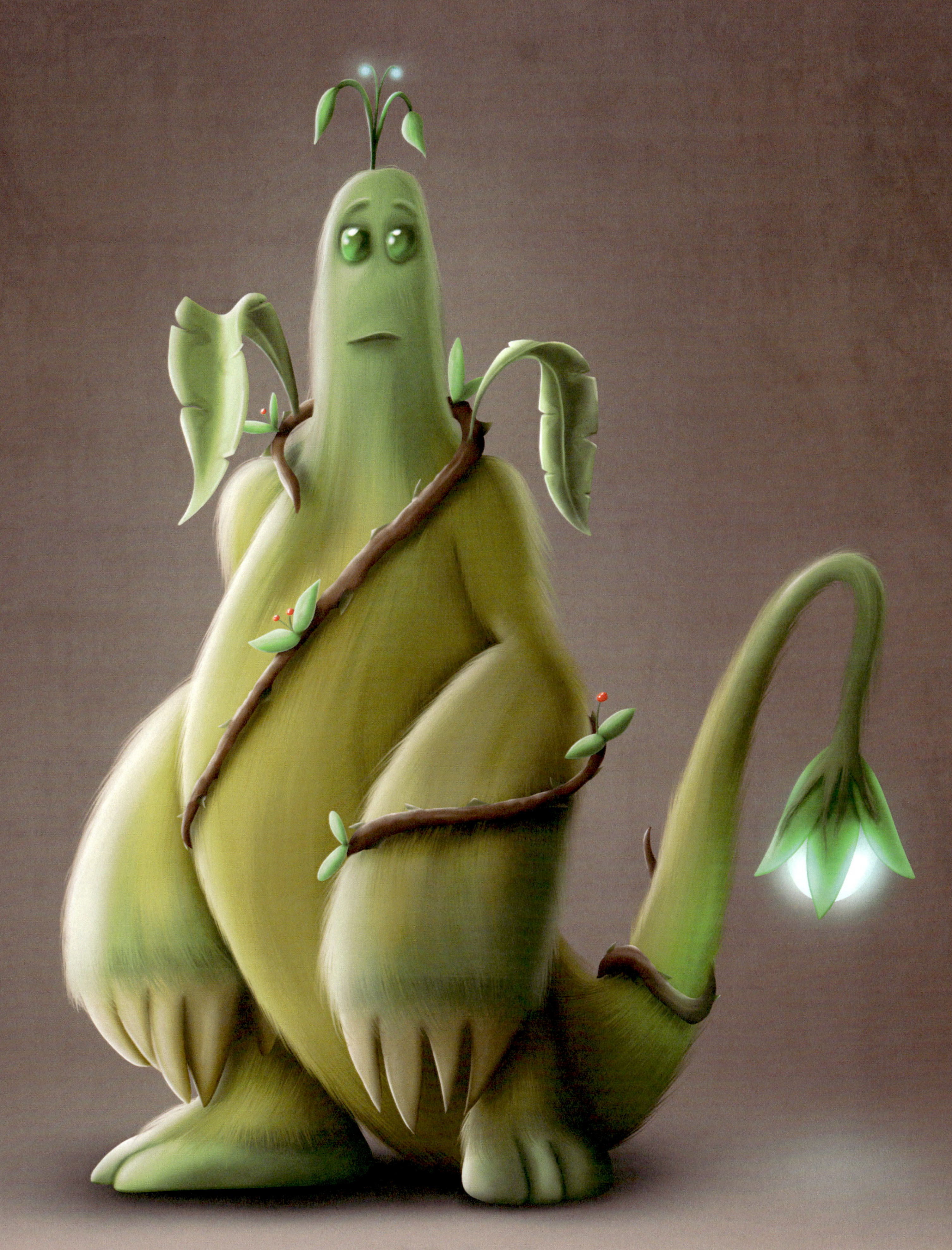

www.deltakosh.com